IMMANUEL
IN
OUR PLACE

THE GOSPEL ACCORDING TO THE OLD TESTAMENT

A series of studies on the lives
of Old Testament characters, written for
laypeople and pastors, and designed to
encourage Christ-centered reading, teaching,
and preaching of the Old Testament.

TREMPER LONGMAN III
J. ALAN GROVES

Series Editors

After God's Own Heart, by Mark J. Boda
Crying Out for Vindication, by David R. Jackson
Faith in the Face of Apostasy, by Raymond B. Dillard
From Famine to Fullness, by Dean R. Ulrich
Hope in the Midst of a Hostile World, by George M.
  Schwab
Immanuel In Our Place, by Tremper Longman III
Living in the Gap Between Promise and Reality, by
  Iain M. Duguid
Living in the Grip of Relentless Grace, by Iain M. Duguid
Longing for God in an Age of Discouragement, by
  Bryan Gregory
Love Divine and Unfailing, by Michael P. V. Barrett
Right in Their Own Eyes, by George M. Schwab
Salvation Through Judgment and Mercy, by
  Bryan D. Estelle

IMMANUEL
IN
OURPLACE

SEEING CHRIST IN
ISRAEL'S WORSHIP

TREMPER LONGMAN III

PUBLISHING
P.O.BOX 817 • PHILLIPSBURG • NEW JERSEY 08865-0817

Page design by Tobias Design
Typesetting by Michelle Feaster

Printed in the United States of America

Library of Congress Cataloging-in-Publication Data

Longman, Tremper.
    Immanuel in our place : seeing Christ in Israel's worship / Tremper Longman III.
        p. cm. — (The Gospel according to the Old Testament)
    Includes bibliographical references and index.
    ISBN-10: 0-87552-651-9 (pbk.)
    ISBN-13: 978-0-87552-651-5 (pbk.)
    1. Public worship in the Bible. 2. Bible. O.T.—Criticism, interpretation, etc. 3. Bible. O.T.—Relation to the New Testament. 4. Bible. N.T.—Relation to the Old Testament. I. Title. II. Series.

BS1199.P93 L66 2001
264—dc21

2001033925

CONTENTS

FOREWORD

The New Testament is in the Old concealed;
the Old Testament is in the New revealed.
                    —Augustine

Concerning this salvation, the prophets, who spoke of the grace that was to come to you, searched intently and with the greatest care, trying to find out the time and circumstances to which the Spirit of Christ in them was pointing when he predicted the sufferings of Christ and the glories that would follow. It was revealed to them that they were not serving themselves but you, when they spoke of the things that have now been told you by those who have preached the gospel to you by the Holy Spirit sent from heaven. Even angels long to look into these things. (1 Peter 1:10–12 NIV)

"In addition, some of our women amazed us. They went to the tomb early this morning but didn't find his body. They came and told us that they had seen a vision of angels, who said he was alive. Then some of our companions went to the tomb and found it just as the women had said, but him they did not see." He said to them, "How foolish you are, and how slow of heart to believe all that the prophets have spoken! Did not the Christ have to suffer these things and then enter his glory?" And beginning with Moses and all the Prophets, he explained to them what was said in all the Scriptures concerning himself. (Luke 24:22–27 NIV)

The prophets searched. Angels longed to see. And the disciples didn't understand. But Moses, the prophets, and all the Old Testament Scriptures had spoken about it— that Jesus would come, suffer, and then be glorified. God began to tell a story in the Old Testament, the ending for which the audience eagerly anticipated. But the Old Testament audience was left hanging. The plot was laid out but the climax was delayed. The unfinished story begged an ending. In Christ, God has provided the climax to the Old Testament story. Jesus did not arrive unannounced; his coming was declared *in advance* in the Old Testament, not just in explicit prophecies of the Messiah but by means of the stories of all of the events, characters, and circumstances in the Old Testament. God was telling a larger, overarching, unified story. From the account of creation in Genesis to the final stories of the return from exile, God progressively unfolded his plan of salvation. And the Old Testament account of that plan always pointed in some way to Christ.

AIMS OF THIS SERIES

The Gospel According to the Old Testament Series is committed to the proposition that the Bible, both Old and New Testaments, is a unified revelation of God, and that its thematic unity is found in Christ. The individual books of the Old Testament exhibit diverse genres, styles, and individual theologies, but tying them all together is the constant foreshadowing of, and pointing forward to, Christ. Believing in the fundamentally Christocentric nature of the Old Testament, as well as the New Testament, we offer this series of studies in the Old Testament with the following aims:

- to lay out the pervasiveness of the revelation of Christ in the Old Testament
- to promote a Christ-centered reading of the Old Testament
- to encourage Christ-centered preaching and teaching from the Old Testament

To this end, the volumes in this series are written for pastors and laypeople, not scholars.

While such a series could take a number of different shapes, we have decided, in most cases, to focus individual volumes on Old Testament figures—people—rather than books or themes. Some books, of course, will receive major attention in connection with their authors or main characters (e.g., Daniel or Isaiah). Also, themes will be emphasized in connection with particular figures.

It is our hope and prayer that this series will revive interest in and study of the Old Testament as readers recognize that the Old Testament points forward to Jesus Christ.

TREMPER LONGMAN III
J. ALAN GROVES

PREFACE

The Old Testament is hard for Christians to understand and appreciate. While the New Testament presents the words and actions of Christ, the Old Testament seems to offer a harsh and bloody religion. Elsewhere I have dealt with this perception of a radical difference between the two testaments in general terms,[1] but our present topic, the priestly theology of the Old Testament, brings it to the fore once again.

The priestly theology of the Old Testament appears to us at first glance as elitist and violent. Our worship experience is quite distant from the blood of numerous sacrifices performed by ornately dressed priests in a specifically designated holy place on certain consecrated days. On closer examination, though, we will gain profound theological insight and practical wisdom by studying these ancient priestly texts. Indeed, among many other things, we will come to a deeper appreciation and comprehension of the most important redemptive act of all, Jesus' death on the cross. After all, even a cursory reading of the Gospels and Epistles reveals that the significance of Jesus' death is painted in the colors of the tabernacle, priesthood, festivals, and sacrifices of the Old Testament.

But even before we explore the christological dimensions of the priestly theology of the Old Testament, we will learn more about the nature of God and our relationship with him. We will see that God is our heavenly King who establishes his rulership in the midst of his people. As King, he consecrates space, people, certain acts, and times that are especially dedicated to his service. We now turn our attention to these important though difficult and not infrequently neglected concepts from the Old Testament. We look first at sacred space, then sacred actions, then sacred people, and finally sacred time.

This book is part of a series that began with a book by Raymond B. Dillard. The series itself commemorates his life and work. I wish to dedicate this book to him. My career began with his encouragement, and he mentored me in my writing and teaching. We are now nearing the eighth anniversary of his death, but his influence is still very much felt by me and countless others.

I also want to thank my good friend and former colleague Alan Groves, chairman of the Old Testament department at Westminster Theological Seminary in Philadelphia. Al gave me much good advice in the writing of this book, and I deeply appreciate it.

Thom Notaro of P&R Publishing gave the manuscript a very thorough reading at the final editorial stage and offered excellent advice on style and substance.

However, I did not accept all of my readers' suggestions, and thus, not surprisingly, they do not share all of my conclusions. I am, for good or ill, the one responsible for the final content.

PART ONE

SACRED SPACE

God, the King, created sacred space for his presence on earth. The following section explores this idea of sacred space in the Old Testament. This concept should strike us, living after the death and resurrection of Jesus, as a strange idea. After all, today we can meet with God anywhere and anytime. However, this generous access to God was not the case during the time between the expulsion from Eden and the accomplishment of Christ's great redemptive acts. What does it mean that a particular location was set aside as holy? How does this concept develop throughout the Old Testament? These are the questions that occupy our attention in the following pages.

I

PARADISE GAINED AND LOST:
SACRED SPACE
FROM THE BEGINNING

✦⋮✦

Genesis 2[1] narrates the creation story a second time. It does not contradict the first but rather retells the account of creation with a new focus. Genesis 1 describes the creation of the cosmos; Genesis 2 focuses on the creation of humanity, the apex of God's good work.

The manner of creation of Adam, the male, illustrates his special place in God's universe. He was created from the dust of the ground. In other words, he connected with the creation. Like the animals and the earth itself, he was a creature. But there is more. He came to life when God breathed breath into his nostrils. He had a special relationship with the Creator! The creation process itself emphasizes humanity's glory as the very climax of God's work of creation. God's method for creating Eve shows that her special place in creation was the equal of Adam's. She was formed, not from his head or from his feet, but from his side—her very creation showing her equal status with the man. She was to be his "helper." In the Hebrew Bible, this is not a term of subservience, but one indicating that she was his "ally." After all, God himself is called the "helper" of humanity (Pss. 30:10; 54:4; Heb. 13:6).

This point is doubly highlighted when we contrast the creation of the first man according to Genesis 2 with the creation of the first human beings according to Mesopotamian tradition. True, in both the recipe starts with dust or clay, the very earth itself, but it is with the second ingredient that the difference is clearly seen. And here we have variation in Mesopotamian tradition. In the *Enuma Elish*,[2] humanity's dust is mixed with the blood of a demon god killed for his treachery against the second generation of gods. Humans are demons from their creation. According to *Atrahasis*,[3] the second ingredient is the spit of the gods, a far cry from the glorious breath of the Creator! The creation process according to Mesopotamian tradition fits well with the overall low view of humanity professed by that culture. After all, according again to *Atrahasis*, humans were created with the express purpose of relieving the lesser gods from the arduous labor of digging irrigation ditches. On the other hand, the Genesis account conforms well to the high view of Scripture concerning humanity. Human beings, male and female, were created in the image of God (Gen. 1:26–27).

What does it mean to be created in the image of God? Theologians have alternatively scratched their heads and fought viciously over that question. Often the answer boils down to what the theologian believes separates us as human beings from the rest of creation. Such an approach has often resulted in a focus on human rationality: it is our reason that reflects God. But that approach is dangerous on a number of levels. Perhaps most worrisome is the tendency to promote the interests of reason over other important aspects of personality, such as emotions and imagination. With such a view, we also put too much trust in human reason.

A better approach is to ask how images functioned in

the ancient Near East. In a word, images represented their objects. The best example comes from the realm of royalty. In antiquity, kings would create images of themselves and set them up all around their kingdom to remind the people of their authority and presence. God created human beings in such a way that they too represented God's presence on earth. Human beings reflect God's glory in a way that no other part of God's creation does.

To summarize, human beings are the apex of God's creation according to Genesis 1–2. They were the climax of the creation process; they were created in the image of God.

SACRED SPACE CREATED

These special creatures, Adam and Eve, were placed in a very special location, the garden of Eden.[4] The garden was a perfect place for humankind to live; it supplied every need. It was lush with plants, including fruits. It was well watered, with four rivers running from it. The garden was truly a paradise, though the Hebrew word related to paradise (*pardes,* which means "park" or "forest" or "orchard") is never used in the Bible in connection with Eden. "Eden" itself most likely means "abundance," again showing its luxurious character.[5] Indeed, Eden was the "garden of God," according to Ezekiel 31:8. Ezekiel also describes Eden as a mountain (28:14). Whether we are to read back into Genesis this description of Ezekiel is a matter of debate. It could be a later theological/literary image rather than a physical description. Nonetheless, the connection of garden and mountain will prove an important one for the development of the biblical theme of holy place.

Eden's utopian nature, however, was not primarily a function of its physical benefits. Perfect relationship filled that function. In the first place, the relationship between God and his human creatures was harmonious, personal, and intimate. God walked in the garden (Gen. 3:8); the impression of the text is that God could make his presence known throughout the garden.

As a result of the strong relationship between God and his human creatures, Adam and Eve related well together. This is symbolized by their being naked and feeling no shame in each other's presence. They could be completely vulnerable with each other in the garden—psychologically and spiritually, I would suggest, as well as physically.

The garden was the place where what we know today as the institutions of work and marriage found their origin. The garden would not tend itself, but Adam and Eve were charged with its care. We are led to understand that this work was not arduous, but rather a joy. Nature responded well to Adam and Eve's efforts to tend it. Furthermore, the intimacy between Adam and Eve was formalized in a ritual of leaving-weaving-cleaving that today we would recognize as marriage (Gen. 2:23–25).

Everything was fine in the garden. At its center stood two trees. The first was the tree of life. We are not told much about this tree, and if we wish to say anything, we are left to speculate. But we might argue that Adam and Eve ate from this tree as long as they were in the garden and that it was the fruit of this tree that kept them from dying.

The real focus of attention is on a second tree, the tree of the knowledge of good and evil. God gave Adam and Eve the delicious fruit of many trees, but he prohibited them, on pain of death, from eating the fruit of this tree—no explanation given. What was this tree? This question has vexed interpreters over the years, but a consensus of sorts may be seen between the three leading recent evangelical interpreters of Genesis.[6] In short, this tree represents moral autonomy. Eating of it would mean seeking wisdom apart from a relationship with God, who himself is wisdom. Thus, the name of the tree describes the nature of their rebellious act, their effort to acquire moral autonomy.

Before narrating the events of Genesis 3, however, let me finish this section by emphasizing the theological significance of Eden. In the garden of God, Adam and Eve moved easily in the presence of their Maker. There were no special holy places—there was no need for such. Every place was holy and Adam and Eve themselves were holy. The whole garden was God's sanctuary. But this was soon to change.

THE FALL'S IMPACT: SACRED SPACE LOST

The serpent makes his appearance suddenly at the beginning of Genesis 3 after a brief description of his craftiness. Hebrew narrative is normally sparing in its descriptions of its characters, only introducing character traits that are important to the story. Nonetheless, we cannot help but be left with questions. Where did the serpent come from? Who is he? Why is he God's enemy or at least working against God's purposes?

The book of Genesis provides us with few answers to these questions, but if we expand our purview, as is appropriate considering the organic unity of the Bible (after all, God is the ultimate author of the whole thing), then we can at least recognize the serpent as the Devil himself (Rom. 16:20; Rev. 12:9). The Devil begins his evil work by approaching the woman Eve with a leading question: "Did God really say you must not eat any of the fruit in the garden?" (Gen. 3:1).

We get an immediate example of his craftiness. He knew very well that this is not what God said, and the woman is quick to defend God's command: "Of course we may eat it. . . . It's only the fruit from the tree at the center of the garden that we are not allowed to eat. God says we must not eat of it or even touch it, or we will die" (Gen. 3:3).

Notice, though, that in her zeal to defend God's character she stretches the truth. God did not prohibit touching the tree; only eating its fruit. She, in essence, provides us the first example of "fencing the law"—that is, making human rules that guard us from breaking the divine rule. "If God doesn't want us to get drop-down drunk (compare Prov. 23:29–35), then I won't even have a glass of wine with dinner." This, in spite of the fact that the Bible celebrates wine as God's good gift to his people (Ps. 104:15). The woman, on the brink of her rebellion, shows herself to be the first legalist.

The serpent sees the opening and then attacks God's credibility. "You won't die! . . . God knows that your eyes will be opened when you eat it. You will become just like God, knowing everything, both good and evil" (Gen. 3:4).

This argument convinces Eve, and she eats the fruit. While some think that this makes Eve especially culpable, it should be pointed out how easily Adam follows her lead. At least it took the crafty serpent himself to break down Eve's resistance to eating the fruit. Adam doesn't even question Eve's offer but readily takes a big bite.

The effects are drastic and immediate. Their sin ruptures their relationship. They eat, and they look at each other and notice for the first time that they are naked, and so they cover themselves with fig leaves. In other words, for the first time Adam and Eve feel vulnerable before the gaze of the other person. They feel—indeed they know—that they are inadequate, physically, morally, spiritually. Not wanting to endure the shame and the guilt, they have only one recourse—seek cover. They want to hide from the gaze of the other person. At this moment, alienation settles into human relationships. This account explains why we can feel loneliness even in the closest of human relationships.

As bad as the alienation between Adam and Eve must have been, even worse is the effect on the divine-human relationship. In this case, more than cover is needed. God's presence brings simple flight. When God finally confronts Adam, he admits, "I heard you, so I hid. I was afraid because I was naked" (Gen. 3:10). At this point, the blame shifting starts in earnest. God charges Adam by asking the question: "Have you eaten the fruit I commanded you not to eat?" (v. 11). Adam admits to eating the fruit, but blames Eve. Eve also admits that she ate the fruit but points to Satan.

All three are thus culpable, and so all three receive their punishment, beginning with the serpent, then the woman, and finally the man. The order is the same by which they are introduced into the narrative at the beginning of the chapter.

As for the serpent, the first aspect of its curse is that it will now be reduced to "eating the dust." What is the relationship between a snake and Satan? Does this mean that the primordial snake had legs? If so, what did it look like? These are questions that the Bible does not address and we should be hesitant to answer. Certainly, as later Israelites (and we today) observe a snake slithering along the ground, they (and we) are reminded of Satan's role in the Fall. The most significant part of the curse on the serpent, however, is the resulting enmity between its offspring with the descendants of the woman. This vicious rivalry begins right away as we read the chapters that follow the account of the Fall.

In Genesis 4, we observe how Cain (a descendant of the serpent) mercilessly kills Abel (a descendant of the woman). At the end of Genesis 4 (vv. 17–26), we see a genealogy of the descendants of Cain, followed by a lengthier genealogy of Adam through Seth (the descendants of the woman). As Saint Augustine would state it, from the time of the Fall on, humankind is divided into two parts, a City of Man (following Satan) and the City of God.

In the curse on the serpent, not only is the conflict predicted, but so is the conclusion of the conflict: "He will crush your head, and you will strike his heel" (Gen. 3:15). Here the descendants of the woman are crystallized in one descendant who will destroy the serpent, but at some cost. Though contemporary doubt has clouded the scene, the traditional interpretation that asserts the fulfillment of this promise in the Messiah, Jesus Christ, is surely right. Already, we observe that even in the midst of curse for sin, God provides a way of salvation. This passage has appropriately been called the *protoevangelium* (the gospel before the gospel). We will, in a sense, be following this story throughout this book as we see how God provides a place of worship for the residents of the City of God, a provision that ultimately will lead to Jesus, the serpent crusher.

However, judgment does not end with the serpent. Eve is next, and her curse focuses on the fact that Eve is the mother of relationship. Her womb gives and nourishes life. After the Fall, however, this life-giving role will be fulfilled only with pain and suffering. Furthermore, the relationship that she has with her husband will suffer. She will desire her husband, but he will be her master, according to Genesis 3:16.

Some debate attends the question of what her desire entails. Is it a legitimate desire to be in a relationship that will fail, or is her desire to control her husband and be dominant in the relationship? The rare Hebrew word "desire" (*teshuqah*) is used again in Genesis 4:7, where it is sin that seeks to control Cain, and this use lends strong support to the second interpretive option. In either case, the point is that there will now be a power struggle in a relationship that was divinely intended to be a truly equal partnership.

Lastly, Adam receives his judgment. That judgment focuses on Adam's work. He was charged in Genesis 1:28–31 with the task of maintaining the garden. Now that work will be fraught with futility. He will succeed, as the woman will succeed in having children, but not without sweat, blood, and sorrow. Even his success will be fleeting.

While recognizing the curse on each of the three perpetrators of the crime, we should not lose sight that at heart the very act itself created a situation of great tragedy. Adam and Eve's intimate relationship with God was now broken. They were ejected from the garden, no longer able to have easy access to the divine presence. After all, God is holy and he does not tolerate the presence of sin. However, it is a sign of God's continuing grace that he did not completely sever his relationship with his rebellious human creatures.

GOD'S GRACE: SACRED SPACE PROMISED

Indeed, at this time God could have justly eradicated human beings from existence. After all, he had earlier announced concerning the tree of the knowledge of good and evil, "If you eat of its fruit, you will surely die" (Gen. 2:17). They had eaten the fruit, and God could have immediately exercised his prerogative of executing his creatures. However, in the first of many examples of God's gracious patience, he did not kill them. Certainly, death entered the human experience for the first time. They were ejected from the garden and from access to the tree of life. They were now doomed to die someday, but not before they had children and the human race multiplied.

Indeed, a close study of the major narratives of Genesis 3–11 shows a recurrent pattern that resembles what we have seen in the account of the Fall. Humans sin and God gives a judgment speech, which is followed by a token of God's grace, and then the execution of God's judgment.[7] The token of God's grace in Genesis 3 is his provision of clothes made from animal skins to the human couple (v. 21). This gift acknowledges a continuing alienation in relationship, but along with that it shows God's continuing care for his creatures.

Eden! The garden of God! The mountain garden where God first placed his human creatures. God was there with Adam and Eve, and God's presence made paradise sacred space.

Eden truly was a paradise. Adam and Eve lived in harmony with each other, with creation, and with themselves. Foundationally, they lived in perfect harmony and relationship with God, their Creator. Indeed, the harmony of the garden flowed from their harmony with God. In Eden, there were no special places, no places set apart for communion with God. Rather, the whole of Eden was holy, a sanctuary, if you will. Adam and Eve walked in the garden with God. We are given the impression that there was free and easy access to the presence of God.

Human rebellion destroyed the harmony of the garden. After the Fall, Adam and Eve experienced alienation from each other, from creation, and from themselves. Most foundationally, they experienced alienation from God. They were removed from the garden.

However, God was not done with them. Even in the midst of judgment, God provided a note of hope to them. The enmity that the serpent, Adam, and Eve introduced will one day be resolved (Gen. 3:15). Genesis 3 does not yet formulate it quite this way, but the hope is that one day perhaps Eden will be restored.

Paul very poignantly speaks about hope in a fallen world in Romans 8:18–25:

> Yet what we suffer now is nothing compared to the glory he will give us later. For all creation is waiting eagerly for that future day when God will

reveal who his children really are. Against its will, everything on earth was subjected to God's curse. All creation anticipates the day when it will join God's children in glorious freedom from death and decay. For we know that all creation has been groaning as in the pains of childbirth right up to the present time. And even we Christians, although we have the Holy Spirit within us as a foretaste of future glory, also groan to be released from pain and suffering. We, too, wait anxiously for that day when God will give us our full rights as his children, including the new bodies he has promised us. Now that we are saved, we eagerly look forward to this freedom. For if you already have something, you don't need to hope for it. But if we look forward to something we don't have yet, we must wait patiently and confidently.

As we will see, this longing for a return to Eden will not be satisfied until the very end of time. Nonetheless, God will give his people glimpses of Eden, right from the start. As soon as they leave Eden, God makes his presence known to them. This is the story of the family of God and the altars where they find fellowship with him.

FOR FURTHER REFLECTION

1. Can we still be said to bear the divine image after the Fall?
2. Reflect on your own unfulfilled and frustrated desires. Can they be seen as a "longing" for a return to Eden?
3. Reflect on the times in your life when you feel lonely or have a sense of isolation. How are these thoughts and feelings related to the Fall?

4. Is there any place quite like Eden today?
5. What does it mean that you were created from the dust?
6. What does it mean that you are created in the image of God? How should you treat others created in God's image?

2

ALTARS: OCCASIONAL
TESTIMONIES
TO SACRED SPACE

※※※

After Genesis 3, Adam and Eve's easy access to the presence of God was denied. Sin had entered the picture, and God hates sin. We have seen in the previous chapter that Adam and Eve were ejected from Eden, where they walked freely with God. Nonetheless, God in his grace did provide a way for his people to come to worship and commune with him. In later chapters, we will examine the contents of this worship, but for now we will focus on the question of location. In what kind of place did God's people worship him right after the Fall?

GOD'S PRESENCE AND ALTAR BUILDING

The name given to the place of worship between the Fall and the Exodus is the altar. The first express mention of an altar is Genesis 8:20, which tells of an object built by Noah after the flood waters receded, where he offered sacrifices to the Lord. However, we should not assume that this is the very first altar. From their actions in Genesis 4:3–5, we may assume that Cain and Abel brought their sacrifices to an altar.

But what is an altar? An altar is a simple structure built of earth or stone marking the place where God meets people. Typically, God made his presence known at a location and then commanded his people to build an altar there. We will later see that altars were incorporated into the larger sanctuaries, the tabernacle and the temple, but before Moses the altar was the only architectural feature marking a place as holy.

The Hebrew word translated "altar" is *mizbeah*, formed from the verbal root *zabah*, which means "sacrifice" or "slaughter." Though it is dangerous to rely exclusively on the etymology of a word for its meaning, the idea of sacrifice is supported by the use of the word in biblical contexts. It appears that the altar was a place where sacrifice could and did take place. The altar was where the worshiper came into the presence of God, and God, as we have seen, hates sin. Therefore, sin had to be accounted for before a person entered the holy place. We will later look at this in more detail, but the most obvious function of sacrifice was to atone for sin. Thus, it is not at all surprising that at the heart of the altar was the idea of sacrifice.

We may further appeal to other Scripture passages to help us understand the nature of altars. Though written much later, the so-called altar law in Exodus 20:24–26 appears to reflect earlier times as well as later times.

> The altars you make for me must be simple altars of earth. Offer on such altars your sacrifices to me—your burnt offerings and peace offerings, your sheep and goats and your cattle. Build altars in the places where I remind you who I am, and I will come and bless you there. If you build altars from stone, use only uncut stones. Do not chip or shape the stones with a tool, for that would make them unfit for holy use. And you may not approach my altar by steps. If you do, someone may

look up under the skirts of your clothing and see your nakedness.

This passage deserves lengthy commentary, but for our purpose we will only point out a few relevant points. In the first place, this law implies the construction of multiple altars. Indeed, it would not be until the building of the temple that worship would be restricted to a single altar located in that structure.

Second, the altar was to be simple, not ornate. This feature was probably to distinguish it from more ornate altars of the pagan Canaanites. Other aspects of this law also distance the worship of the Israelites from the Canaanites, most notably the prohibition of steps so that not even a hint of the sexual rituals of the Canaanites may occur at the Israelite altar.

We can also observe that the altar was a place of sacrifice. Animals were to be slaughtered on the altar. After all, those individuals who would come into the presence of God at an altar were sinners who themselves deserved death (see especially chap. 7).

But most importantly, the altar was a holy place, a set-apart place, because that was where God chose to meet with his people and bring them his blessings.

NOAH'S ALTAR

That the altar was a place of sacrifice as well as a place where God made his presence known to his people may be seen in the very first mentioned altar, that of Noah after the flood (Gen. 8:20). Again, it is important to remember that, though this passage is the first explicit mention of an altar, it is highly improbable that it was the first altar. An altar is presupposed by the action of Genesis 4:3–4 describing the sacrifices that Cain and Abel brought to God. However, we can get a clear view of the role of an altar by looking at the occasion on which Noah built one.

The context of the building of Noah's altar is the flood story. Due to the excessive sin of humans, God determined to judge them by means of a flood. Always gracious, even in the context of judgment, God extended his grace to Noah (Gen. 8:1) and told him to build an ark. After the waters receded, Noah disembarked from his ark, and his very first action was to build the altar and offer sacrifices on it.

Noah, after all, had just survived an incredible ordeal. All of humanity had just been destroyed in God's judgment and only he and his immediate family survived among the creatures God created in his image. Noah's immediate reaction was what we would expect from a man who had been the recipient of God's grace—gratitude. Noah built an altar, which created a holy place, a sanctuary, where he could come into the presence of God. He then offered sacrifices to God. The specific type of sacrifice that he offered was burnt offerings (*'olah*). We will later see that this particular kind of sacrifice was the foundational sacrifice that both made atonement for one's sin and provided a gift from the worshiper to God (see chap. 7). In short, Noah's building an altar was the first step in his act of worship by which he began the new phase of his life after the horrible flood waters.

THE ALTARS OF THE PATRIARCHS

The patriarchs were men whom God chose to provide the foundation for Israel, his chosen people. Genesis 1–11, the primeval history, has a worldwide focus. After the Fall, the history of humanity is marked by continual sin, followed by God's judgment and continuing grace. In Genesis 12, the narrative focus narrows on one individual, Abram, who would later receive the name Abraham.

God chose him to be the foundation of a new people. He desired now to reach humanity through this man and his descendants. As such, God placed a demand on him: "Leave your country, your relatives, and your father's house, and go to the land that I will show you" (Gen. 12:1). In return, God gave him a manifold promise:

> I will cause you to become the father of a great nation. I will bless you and make you famous, and I will make you a blessing to others. I will bless those who bless you and curse those who curse you. All the families of the earth will be blessed through you. (vv. 2–3)

These great promises reverberate not only through Genesis and the rest of the Pentateuch, but through the entirety of Scripture.[1] Because he was the recipient of the promises and the foundation of the nation of Israel, Abraham is called a patriarch, a father. The narrative that describes his life flows naturally into the narrative about his son Isaac and his grandson Jacob. They too are called patriarchs in tradition and are often linked together in later Old Testament tradition.

When Abraham arrived in the promised land, he worshiped God. Not surprisingly, he built altars as he traveled through the land. As a matter of fact, his first recorded act after entering the promised land was to build an altar. Shechem in the northern hill country was his first recorded stopping point. At that place, according to Genesis 12:7, God appeared to him and reiterated the promise that he would give Abraham the land. In response, Abraham "built an altar there to commemorate the LORD's visit." The altar is built at a place where God made his special presence known.

Abraham received the promise, but not the land. In response to Abraham's wavering faith in the fulfillment of the promise, God assured him that the land would come to his descendants but many years would pass before that would actually happen:

> You can be sure that your descendants will be strangers in a foreign land, and they will be oppressed as slaves for four hundred years. But I will punish the nation that enslaves them, and in the end they will come away with great wealth. (But you will die in peace, at a ripe old age.) After four generations your descendants will return here to this land, when the sin of the Amorites has run its course. (Gen. 15:13–16)

Abraham, though a powerful man, was also a resident alien in the land. He moved from place to place. As he did, he constructed altars wherever he was in order to worship the Lord and commemorate the Lord's presence at that place. As we follow the narrative, we see that he built altars not only at Shechem but also between Bethel and Ai (Gen. 12:8; also 13:4), in Hebron (13:18), and on a mountain in the region of Moriah (22:9). His grandson Jacob is also described as building an altar at Bethel (35:1–7).

The result of all this building was that the landscape of the promised land was dotted with altars. These altars indicated places where God appeared to his people, who would ultimately inherit the land. In a sense, it was like planting a flag and claiming the land in the name of Yahweh.

Before we leave the subject of the patriarchal altars, we need to point out an important characteristic of their description. Two times Abraham's altars are said to be built next to trees. First of all, Genesis 12:6 reports, "Traveling through Canaan, they came to a place near Shechem and set up camp beside the oak of Moreh." Then in connection with the altar in Hebron we read, "Then Abram moved his camp to the oak grove owned by

Mamre, which is at Hebron. There he built an altar to the LORD" (Gen. 13:18).

The narratives are selective in their description, so we need to be careful about how far we press this evidence. It is conceivable, though, that it was Abraham's common practice to build the altar near a prominent tree or grove of trees.

In the first place, we should record that this practice was potentially dangerous in that it might lead to a false form of worship. After all, the Canaanites had a fertility religion and often constructed their ritual places near trees. However, the assumption of the biblical narrative is that God directed Abraham to build his altars in these locations.

We thus need to ask, What is the significance of the connection between places of worship and trees? The answer, though not explicit in the text, is fairly obvious, I believe, and will become more so as we continue our discussion of the place of worship. The tree next to the place where God meets his human servants reminds us of the garden of Eden. It is not the garden, but it evokes the garden. It is a little bit of Eden in a fallen world.

EXCURSUS: THE SPECIAL PRESENCE OF GOD

The Bible makes it very clear that God is everywhere. Unlike human beings, he is not restricted to one location. Psalm 139 expresses this thought very powerfully:

> I can never escape from your spirit!
>> I can never get away from your presence!
> If I go up to heaven, you are there;
>> if I go down to the place of the dead, you are
>>> there.
> If I ride the wings of the morning,
>> if I dwell by the farthest oceans,

even there your hand will guide me,
and your strength will support me.
I could ask the darkness to hide me
and the light around me to become night—
but even in darkness I cannot hide from you.
To you the night shines as bright as day.
Darkness and light are both alike to you.
(Ps. 139:7–12)

Theologians use the term "omnipresence" to refer to this biblical truth. God is everywhere in his creation, as Jeremiah reminds us: " 'Am I a God who is only in one place?' asks the LORD. 'Do they think I cannot see what they are doing? Can anyone hide from me? Am I not everywhere in all the heavens and earth?' asks the LORD" (Jer. 23:23–24).

God's omnipresence is closely related to the biblical teaching that God is a spirit. In answer to the woman at the well, Jesus teaches that "God is Spirit, so those who worship him must worship in spirit and in truth" (John 4:24). As Spirit, he does not have a body that would restrict his location to one place. Not surprisingly, the Bible teaches that God is invisible, as in 1 Timothy 1:17: "Glory and honor to God forever and ever. He is the eternal King, the unseen one who never dies; he alone is God. Amen."

Even though God is omnipresent, the Bible also teaches that God is present in a special way in certain locations. There is a sense in which we can say that God is present in heaven but absent from hell. He is present with Christians but absent from nonbelievers. Some theologians call this latter sense the special presence of God. God is not only present in being, but his presence is perceived in a definite way. This presence may be to judge or to bless.

We can immediately understand how the teaching about God's presence is crucial for the issue we are discussing. We understand the Bible to say that God makes his presence known in a special way at sanctuaries, whether the sanctuary is an altar as during the period of time until Moses, or the tabernacle/temple during the rest of the Old Testament era. Of course, this question will take on new significance when we consider the presence of God in the person of Jesus Christ.

FOR FURTHER REFLECTION

1. How would you describe to a friend in your own language the idea of God's special presence?
2. Can you describe in your own language the basic form of an Old Testament altar?
3. Are there special holy places today?
4. Are there any modern analogies to an Old Testament altar? Does your church have an altar? Why?
5. Do you have special places where you go to pray or meditate? If not, why not? If yes, then why do you seek them out?

3

THE TABERNACLE OF MOSES:
SACRED SPACE
FOR THE LONG HAUL

A pivotal moment in the history of God's relationship with his people took place on Mount Sinai during the wanderings in the wilderness. God had just freed the Israelites from slavery in Egypt and rescued them from the hand of an angry Pharaoh at the Red Sea. He then directed them to go to Mount Sinai where he would reveal himself to his people through Moses in an even more profound way.

When we think of the revelation of God at Mount Sinai, we think most readily of the covenant that God made with these people. This covenant did not make the old covenant(s) obsolete, but enhanced the relationship the Israelites had with their God. In essence, Mount Sinai was the moment when the family of God became the nation of God. The descendants of Abraham had become a numerous people in keeping with the promise God had made to the patriarch in Genesis 12:2–3:

> I will cause you to become the father of a great
> nation. I will bless you and make you famous,
> and I will make you a blessing to others. I will

bless those who bless you and curse those who curse you. All the families of the earth will be blessed through you.

THE TABERNACLE SUPPLANTS ALTARS

As a nation, God gave them a law to guide their behavior. That law had as its capstone the Ten Commandments, from which all the other laws of the covenant code followed. But more to the point of our topic, as a nation Israel needed a place to come into the presence of God to offer sacrifice and to worship. No longer would small, simple altars be enough; something larger and grander was needed. And for that reason, God told Moses on Sinai, "I want the people of Israel to build me a sacred residence where I can live among them" (Exod. 25:8). With these words, God initiated the building of the tabernacle.

The tabernacle replaced the altar as the primary location where God revealed his intimate presence to his people. More correctly, the tabernacle incorporated the altar since, as we will observe below, the sacrificial altar was an important component of the tabernacle complex. However, as T. Fretheim rightly comments, with the tabernacle we move from the "occasional appearance of God" to God's "ongoing presence" with the community.[1] As we might expect, the tabernacle, like the ark before it, also alluded to the original creation (see below) and specifically to the garden of Eden (see chap. 5, on the menorah).

GOD PLANS THE BUILDING OF HIS DWELLING PLACE

Before proceeding with a description of the tabernacle, it is important to dwell on the significance of the fact that it was God, not Moses, who initiated the building of his sanctuary. God not only told Moses to build it; he gave him specific instructions that he was to follow in every detail: "You must make this Tabernacle and its furnishings exactly according to the plans I will show you" (Exod. 25:9).

God does not leave it to human beings to define the type of worship they will offer him. God knows what is best and he told Moses in detail. The very structure of the second half of Exodus reinforces this point. From Exodus 25:10 through 30:38, God gives instructions to Moses about how to build the sanctuary. Furthermore, in 31:1–11, God appoints two men, Bezalel and Oholiab, to be the leaders of the building project. God further is the one who gave them the wisdom they needed to perform their work. The last chapters of Exodus describe the fulfillment of the divine instructions in detail, thereby recording that the tabernacle indeed conformed to the divine plan (see Exod. 36:8–40:33).

To be sure, the people had an important role to play in the construction of the tabernacle. They even supplied the materials needed to build such an ornate structure. At God's direction, this is what the people supplied: ". . . gold, silver, and bronze; blue, purple, and scarlet yarn; fine linen; goat hair for cloth; tanned ram skins and fine goatskin leather; acacia wood; olive oil for the lamps; spices for the anointing oil and the fragrant incense; onyx stones, and other stones to be set in the ephod and the chestpiece" (Exod. 25:3–7; cf. their presentation of these items in 35:4–35).

But even here notice something crucially important. Where did these items come from? Granted we are left by the biblical text to speculate a little, but it is clear that they did not find these in the wilderness. It is equally safe to assume that they did not amass these materials during their years of slavery in Egypt. No, there is only one possible answer to this question according to the Bible.

These precious materials were given to the Israelites by the Egyptians just before they left. "The LORD caused the Egyptians to look favorably on the Israelites, and they gave the Israelites whatever they asked for. So, like a victorious army, they plundered the Egyptians!" (Exod. 12:36).

The people did not earn these materials by their hard labor or through military means. God moved the hearts of the Egyptians—whether out of respect or out of fear—to simply hand over the goods. God not only gave the plans for the tabernacle; in a very real sense he also provided the materials to build it.

WHAT DID THE TABERNACLE LOOK LIKE?

When we read the book of Exodus, we cannot help but see the importance of the tabernacle. Of the three important topics of the book—the other two being the Exodus and the law—the vast majority of the book (25:1–31:8 and 35:1–40:38) deals with the tabernacle.[2] But what was the tabernacle?

In a word, the tabernacle was a tent; indeed, at places it is called the Tent of Meeting (Exod. 38:8, 30).[3] However, the tabernacle was no simple tent, but rather an ornate structure. The best descriptions in the Bible leave us with some questions of detail. But we can get an adequate picture from Exodus 26, where God commands Moses to build the tabernacle and gives him instructions that allow us to reconstruct its architecture. The summary below also finds support in Exodus 38:9–20, where the execution of God's instructions is narrated.

Most of the description is devoted to the sheets that overlay the tabernacle. There were four layers of sheets, and the instructions start from the inside and work out. The innermost layer was the most ornate. It was "fine linen. . . . decorated with blue, purple, and scarlet yarn, with figures of cherubim skillfully embroidered into them" (Exod. 26:1). This layer was the one visible from within the tabernacle. The interior probably was dimly lit by the menorah (see chap. 5). The air inside the tabernacle was often cloudy from incense and the smoke of sacrifices, the latter coming in from the outside. Nonetheless, as one stood in the tabernacle and looked around, he would see a deep blue background with images of cherubim looking as though suspended in midair.

We will return to this scene later, because it is central to the symbolic field of the tabernacle. But it is hard to miss the idea that the impression was to be a heavenly one. As one walked into the tabernacle, he would be symbolically transferred from an earthly location to a (symbolically at least) heavenly one.

This innermost layer was to be constructed of ten sheets of linen, in two sets of five, with each set bound to the other by fifty gold clasps. Each of the ten sheets was forty-two feet long and six feet wide. Since the next three layers were to cover this very ornate linen sheet, they were longer, made of eleven sheets. These three layers were much more weather resistant, and their main function was likely to protect the innermost layer. From inside to outside, the three more practical layers were sheets of goat hair, followed by ram skin, followed by goat skin. There is a debate concerning the exact nature of the outermost layer. Some take the reference to mean the hide of the sea cow. (The dugong, the dolphin, and the porpoise have all been suggested.) In any case, the outermost layers were more rugged and served to protect the structure and its contents. These three outer layers were also bound together by bronze clasps, rather than gold.

The layers were supported by posts made of precious acacia wood. These posts were fifteen feet high, thus measuring the height of the ceiling inside. The posts all had silver bases and were further joined by crossbars made of acacia overlaid with gold. This describes the tent itself.

Inside the tent was a curtain made of the same ornate material as the innermost curtain. It served to separate the Holy of Holies from other parts of the tabernacle. As we will see in chapter 5, much of the furniture of the tabernacle—most notably the ark of the covenant—was placed behind the curtain. The entrance of the tabernacle proper, always facing east, was to be made of the same special material.

The above summary of Exodus 26 describes the tabernacle proper. Exodus 27:9–21 tells us about the courtyard. It was a large area marked off by curtains of fine, presumably white, linen. The curtains were hung on a series of bronze posts that had bronze bases. The area was bounded by curtains on the north and south that measured 150 feet, while on the east and west they were seventy-five feet long. Like the tabernacle itself, the entrance to the courtyard faced east and was marked by a special curtain made from fine linen and decorated with "beautiful embroidery in blue, purple, and scarlet yarn" (27:16). Such an entrance would draw attention to itself and offer a foretaste of the heavenly realities inside.

THE SYMBOLISM OF THE TENT

As we have already noted, God was deeply concerned that Moses follow his instructions to the letter as the Israelites built the tabernacle and its contents. The author of the book of Hebrews informs us why this was so important:

> They serve in a place of worship that is only a copy, a shadow of the real one in heaven. For when Moses was getting ready to build the Tabernacle, God gave him this warning: "Be sure that

you make everything according to the design I
have shown you here on the mountain" (Heb. 8:5).

The reason why such care had to be taken with the
construction of the tabernacle is that its very structure
and the material out of which it was built reflected heavenly realities. This passage becomes our motivation for
asking about the symbolic value of the tabernacle. What
does it all mean? In God's wisdom, he did not tell us explicitly, but soon we will observe that the answer is fairly
obvious, as well as marvelous.

It is not surprising that Bible readers have let their
imaginations run wild when considering the meaning of
the tabernacle. One illustration is a popular book by Paul
Kiene entitled *The Tabernacle of God in the Wilderness of
Sinai*.[4] There's no need to do a full analysis of this book,
which is quite useless for helping us understand the tabernacle. I will just present a couple of examples of his approach to the meaning of the tabernacle.

We have observed how the tabernacle used a linen of
special quality and color for the innermost curtain, as
well as for crucial points of transition: from the outside
world to the courtyard, then from the courtyard into the
tabernacle per se, and then from the Holy Place to the
Holy of Holies. Kiene remarks that there are four colors
in this special curtain: blue, purple, scarlet, and white.
From almost out of nowhere, he conjectures, "The four
colors may correspond to the four evangelists. Each color
conforms to one of the conspicuously glorious characteristics of the Lord Jesus that the Holy Spirit desires to emphasize in these divine documents."[5] The color blue, he
says, stands for the gospel of John. Kiene speculates that
blue is the color of heaven, and since John gives us a
heavenly portrait of God, then the blue of the special curtain is to be associated with John.

A perhaps even more outlandish example is his understanding of the symbolic value of the wide entrance to

the courtyard. It is twenty cubits, or thirty feet across. This leads to the following interpretation: "Its width is of an inviting size: a full 20 cubits. The Lord Jesus Christ stands before us, so to speak, with outstretched arms and with encouraging, alluring words: 'Come unto me, all ye that labour and are heavy laden, and I will give you rest' " (Matt. 11:28).[6]

Careful readers will wonder where Kiene came up with these interpretations. The connections he draws are arbitrary. They are allegorical in the negative sense, in that they impose a meaning not implied by the text itself. There are allegories that are not speculative but intended by an author, as is obvious from the context.[7] Unfortunately, many people find mysterious interpretations too enticing to pass up, and they accept fanciful views on the author's word. But there is a better way, with far richer results.

THE TABERNACLE AS THE PRESENCE OF GOD ON EARTH

We have already described the idea of God's special presence. God is everywhere, to be sure, but he is present in a special way in particular locations. During the Old Testament time period the faithful would go to certain locations in order to meet God in worship. The tabernacle was such a place, and the symbolism of the entire structure revolved around that one central idea: the Holy God was present in the midst of the camp.[8]

This central truth is supported by the description of the tabernacle in three ways: its structure, its location in the camp, and the materials out of which it is made.

The Tabernacle's Structure and Location

The tabernacle complex itself had three parts, dividing the larger wandering camp of Israelites into four parts. We start at the apex, the Holy of Holies. This place was set apart from the Holy Place by a thick inner curtain. We have already commented on the fact that the furniture, most notably the ark of the covenant, was found in the Holy of Holies. Chapter 5 will discuss the ark in detail, but we can note here that nothing symbolized God's presence on earth as intensely as the ark. That is why it was divided from the rest of the tabernacle, indeed the rest of the world.

The next area out from the center was the Holy Place of the tabernacle, then there was the courtyard, and then the Israelite camp proper. That was the world of Israel. We can complete our picture of the world by mentioning a fifth realm, the area "outside the camp."

As a matter of fact, the tabernacle was to be placed in the center of the camp, surrounded by the tribes of Israel. In this way, God's tent, the tabernacle, was like the tent of any ancient Near Eastern monarch. The king's tent was always in the center, surrounded by his people. This was true not only of a nomadic people, but of an advanced culture like the Assyrians or Babylonians, when their king was on the march with the army. Later we will have occasion to see that the biblical conception of Israel during the wilderness period was that of an army on the march to battle. As such, Israel's King, Yahweh, would camp in the center.

The Materials of the Tabernacle

The type and placement of the materials used to construct the tabernacle reinforce in a dramatic way the central idea of the symbolism of the tabernacle: God was present in the midst of Israel. Exodus 25:3-7 lists these materials: "gold, silver, and bronze; blue, purple, and scarlet yarn; fine linen; goat hair for cloth; tanned ram skins and fine goatskin leather; acacia wood. . . ."

Every one of these materials was expensive and precious indeed. More to our point, however, was the relative location of these items in the construction of the tabernacle. Close reading will show that there was a transition from less precious to more precious materials as one moved from the outside parameter to the Holy of Holies. Bronze was used for the posts of the outermost curtain, but bronze gave way to silver, then to gold, and ultimately to fine gold, used predominately for the furniture in the Holy of Holies. White linen was used on the outer curtain, but eventually this gives way to the fine cloth that was the innermost curtain of the tabernacle. While this served a practical purpose—the less expensive and more utilitarian material on the outside protecting the precious material on the inside—it still reinforced the central symbolic truth of the tabernacle.

We can imagine the presence of God in the Holy of Holies in the tabernacle as a red hot flame. The closer one gets to the center, the hotter it is. Higher degrees of value marked the precious materials used in the tabernacle. There were also decreasing levels of accessibility as one moved from outside the camp to inside the Holy of Holies.

LEVELS OF ACCESSIBILITY OF
THE TABERNACLE

We have described the world as understood by the Pentateuch to be divided into five realms:

1. *Outside the camp:* This was the realm of the Gentile, the ritually unclean; in short, anyone could be outside the camp.
2. *Inside the camp:* Only Israelites who were ritually clean could enter the Israelite camp. In a later chapter, we will show how the priests preserved the purity of the camp by expelling those who infringed on the ritual laws of Israel.

3. *Inside the courtyard:* Though laypeople could enter this area with their sacrificial animals, the courtyard was dominated by the priests and Levites. These men were specially set apart for this task. They performed the sacrifices on behalf of the people, and only they could go further into the tabernacle proper.
4. *Inside the tabernacle:* Here, only the priests and Levites could enter.
5. *Inside the Holy of Holies:* This was the most restricted area of all. Only the high priest could enter this realm, and he could enter it only once a year, during the Day of Atonement (Lev. 16, see below).

THE TABERNACLE AND CREATION

So the tabernacle was heaven on earth. As such it reminds us of the original creation when God's presence was pervasive throughout all of human habitation (Eden). This will be even clearer below when we explore the symbolism of the menorah. For now, however, I would like to point out the well-known connections between the creation of the tabernacle and the creation of the world. This too is a way of making the connection between the tabernacle and Eden, both of which may be described as heaven on earth.

T. Fretheim summarizes the connections between the construction of the tabernacle and the creation by mentioning, for instance, the foundational role of the Holy Spirit in both narratives. The Spirit hovers over the creation according to Genesis 1:2, while Bezalel and the other workers on the tabernacle are given the Spirit to complete their task (Exod. 31:2). Fretheim further notes that God's command to build the tabernacle in Exodus 25–31 may be divided into seven speeches and that the dedication takes place on New Year's Day, the commemoration of the first day of creation (Exod. 40:2, 17). Finally, much as God looks at his creation and pronounces it good, Moses, God's servant, blesses the completed tabernacle structure (Exod. 39:43).[9]

John Levenson expresses the implications of these correspondences when he says,

> The function of these correspondences is to underscore the depiction of the sanctuary as a world, that is, an ordered, supportive, and obedient environment, and the depiction of the world as a sanctuary, that is a place in which the reign of God is visible and unchallenged, and his holiness is palpable, unthreatened, and pervasive.[10]

THE TABERNACLE AND CHRIST

The tabernacle was God's home on earth. It symbolically represented heaven on earth. The total effect of the structure, materials, and location of the tabernacle emphasized that God was present in the midst of the camp.

When we view the tabernacle in terms of God's presence, it becomes obvious how Jesus, our Immanuel ("God with us"), fulfills the role the tabernacle played in the time between Moses and Solomon. However, full development of this theme awaits chapter 6. We need first to examine the temple symbolism. For now, we can only be suggestive by pointing to John 1:14. Most English translations provide a rather bland rendition of this passage: "So the Word became human and lived here on earth among us. He was full of unfailing love and faithfulness. And we have seen his glory, the glory of the only Son of the Father." But the passage comes alive for us when we realize that the verb translated "lived" (*eskēnōsen*) is formed from the noun "tabernacle" (*skēnē*). We feel the force of this verse when we translate it as "the Word . . . tabernacled among us." Jesus is our tabernacle!

FOR FURTHER REFLECTION

1. Describe how an altar and a tabernacle relate to one another.
2. We saw how important it was that God initiated and set the pattern for the tabernacle structure. Are there any parallels to today's worship?
3. God supplied the material needs to build the tabernacle, but today we bring tithes to support the building and maintenance of church buildings and programs. Is this a change?
4. Does the Old Testament, particularly the section about the construction of the tabernacle, have implications for how we build church buildings today?

4

SOLOMON'S TEMPLE:
SACRED SPACE
SETTLED IN THE LAND

G od directed Moses to build the tabernacle because it
was the right structure for the people of God at that
time. It was large enough to accommodate a large
nation, and it was moveable, a crucial feature during a time
when God's people were themselves not settled in the land.

The tabernacle was the center of worship for Israel for
a long period of time. The exact dates of Moses' life are debated, but even if Moses lived as late as the thirteenth century B.C., the tabernacle was an old structure by the time we
reach David's reign soon after the turn of the millennium.

But what's the difference between a tabernacle and a
temple? Why was Solomon the right one to build the temple? And what, if any, changes of symbolism do we see
as we move from tabernacle to temple? These and other
questions will occupy our attention in this chapter.

DAVID, THE WARRIOR, REJECTED
AS TEMPLE BUILDER

One of the most moving stories in the Old Testament
is found in 2 Samuel 7 (1 Chron. 17). God had been good

to David throughout his life. He had raised him from shepherd to king of Israel. He had given him victory in battle so that now he had rest from all his enemies (2 Sam. 7:1). God had even delivered the Jebusite stronghold of Jerusalem into his control, and he had established his capital there. In that capital, he had built a palace made out of the best woods and materials.

As he thought about his life and how good God had been to him, David began to feel guilty about the tabernacle. The kingdom was increasingly stable. David himself was not living in a tent. Why then should God live in a tent? David also likely knew that all the surrounding nations had magnificent temples for their gods. The true and only God of the universe, though, was in a tent, one that may in fact have been showing its age.

David thus made a decision. He would build Yahweh a new and magnificent temple! What could be clearer? Accordingly, he called his prophetic conscience, Nathan, to himself and announced that he would build the temple. Nathan warmly received the idea and encouraged him to proceed. Of course God would approve a plan that honored him so highly.

However, David and Nathan were both wrong. That night God spoke to Nathan and gave him a message for David:

> Go and tell my servant David, "This is what the LORD says. Are you the one to build me a temple to live in? I have never lived in a temple, from the day I brought the Israelites out of Egypt until now. My home has always been a tent, moving from one place to another. And I have never once complained to Israel's leaders, the shepherds of my people Israel. I have never asked them, 'Why haven't you built me a beautiful cedar temple?' " (2 Sam. 7:5–7)

At first, it is not clear what motivated God's rejection of David's plan, but closer reflection leads to two insights into the situation. First, we should remember the tabernacle and why it was built. It was built because God told Moses to build it and gave him exact instructions for its construction. God initiates his own worship. Here David did the initiating, and God did not accept that.

But why didn't God instruct David to build the temple? The answer to this question gives us our first insight into the symbolism of the temple. As we will see shortly, David's son Solomon would be commissioned with the task of building the temple. David himself would spend his life preparing for its construction, but he was not allowed to take part in its actual construction. In 1 Chronicles 22:8, he informs Solomon of the divine reason for prohibiting him from building the temple: ". . . the LORD said to me, 'You have killed many men in the great battles you have fought. And since you have shed so much blood before me, you will not be the one to build a Temple to honor my name.' "

How do we understand this prohibition? Is it because he was an evil man for killing people? Conceivably, it could be a reference to his indirect murder of Uriah. We read about this murder in 2 Samuel 11. Uriah was the husband of Bathsheba, the beautiful woman with whom David slept, even though he knew she was married. This cowardly act occurred during a period when he seemed to shirk his responsibilities as king. The opening sentence of the chapter says, "The following spring, the time of year when kings go to war, David sent Joab and the Israelite army to destroy the Ammonites." In other words, David should have been on the battlefield where he would have stayed out of trouble.

He not only slept with Bathsheba, but he impregnated her and then panicked by trying to cover up his sinful indiscretion. He called Uriah back from the front line and unsuccessfully attempted to coax the husband back into her bed. Finally David resorted to having Joab arrange Uriah's death in battle.

Though this killing was surely a sin, it is very un-likely that God had this act in mind when he prohibited David from building the temple. After all, the reference is to killing many men in battle. And indeed, David killed countless men on the battlefield. Even early in his career the women sang a song about him that caused Saul to grow extremely jealous: "Saul has killed his thousands, and David his ten thousands" (1 Sam. 18:7). Once we un-derstand that these killings are in view, we also under-stand that God's prohibition was not based on an ethical principle. After all, why did David fight all these wars and kill all these soldiers? God instructed him to do so! David was a leader in God's human army. He was the one whom God chose to finish the conquest begun under Joshua.

And here we find the answer to our question. The principle behind the prohibition was not ethical but re-demptive-historical. The temple represented the cessation of the battles of conquest; it symbolized the establishment in the land. David was the conquest completer. He de-feated the last of the inhabitants of the land, most notably the Philistines. As the completer of the conquest, though, he was not going to build the temple. That was left to his son, Solomon, who inherited the land from his father.

Note the significance of Solomon's name. In Hebrew it is pronounced "Shelomo." As we look closely at this name, we see that it is formed from a very common He-brew word with three consonants: sh-l-m. We know this word in its form *shalom*. Solomon would be "Peace." He would represent the period after the conquest. He would be the one whom God chose to build the temple.

GOD CHOOSES THE SITE FOR THE TEMPLE

We have already seen that God directs his own wor-ship. In light of this principle, we are not surprised to observe that God chose the place where the temple was to be built.

But first we need to note an important change from the period of the tabernacle. The tabernacle was a mobile sanctuary, reflecting the reality that God's people had not yet settled in the land. Furthermore, though it was the major sanctuary of the time, it was not the only place of worship. The altar law found in Exodus 20:22–26 was in operation. It assumed the construction of multiple altars in different places.

However, another law of Moses looked into the future and anticipated a time when there would be only one place of worship. This law is found in Deuteronomy 12, and we can get the flavor of it by quoting just a few verses:

> Do not worship the LORD your God in the way these pagan peoples worship their gods. Rather, you must seek the LORD your God at the place he himself will choose from among all the tribes for his name to be honored. There you will bring to the LORD your burnt offerings, your sacrifices, your tithes, your special gifts, your offerings to fulfill a vow, your freewill offerings, and your offerings of the firstborn animals of your flocks and herds. There you and your families will feast in the presence of the LORD your God, and you will rejoice in all you have accomplished because the LORD your God has blessed you. (vv. 4–7)

This law speaks of a single place of worship that the Lord would choose, but it would not happen until after "you drive out the nations that live there" (Deut. 12:2). Interestingly, we hear an echo of this verse in 2 Samuel 7, the chapter where the Lord begins to speak to David about the building of his temple: "When the king was settled in his palace and the LORD had brought peace to the land . . ." (2 Sam. 7:1). Beginning with Solomon, the Israelites were settled in the land; all the internal enemies had been defeated. So it was the appropriate time for the building of the one, central sanctuary.

But where would it be? Again, we see that God determines the answer to this question. In one sense, the story begins in 2 Samuel 24 with its parallel in 1 Chronicles 21. The basic plot of the story is the same in both Samuel and Chronicles. David insists on taking a census in spite of the protests of Joab, who understands that David's actions will have painful consequences. And, sure enough, they do. God is angered with David's census taking. Though the narrative does not explicitly tell us why, we can surmise that David puts his confidence in the number of his fighting men rather than in God the divine warrior.

In any case, God gives David a choice of punishment, and David chooses a plague that lasts three days. As the angel of death is over the threshing floor of a man named Araunah, David prays to God and asks him to stop the killing. God hears his prayers, and David responds by buying the threshing floor and building an altar on the site.

It is not until the report of the building of the temple (see 2 Chron. 3:1–2) that we learn that this later became the site of the temple. It is important to notice that the census story is an unexpected part of the Chronicler's history. After all, the Chronicler's history omits all the other sins of David and Solomon. Chronicles, however, includes it because of its burning interest in matters surrounding the temple.

Looking back to Genesis, we see another very important connection between the earlier history of the people of God and the location of the temple. In 2 Chronicles 3:1 the location is specified as "Mount Moriah." The only other place in Scripture that refers to the mountain by this name is Genesis 22, the account of the binding of

Isaac. In other words, this is the location where God provided the substitute ram for the sacrifice of Abraham's long awaited son.

This connection shows us that God had long intended that the temple would eventually be placed in the vicinity of Jerusalem. Interestingly, the city was only taken by David in the previous generation. Here, though, we can see the wisdom of God in sparing the people an occasion of jealousy. After all, tensions were always present between the northern and southern tribes. If the temple had been placed in one of the tribal allotments, then the fortunate tribe would have had reason to feel superior to the others. But Jerusalem was taken long after the tribal settlement and was "David's city," independent of the tribes in a way that Washington D.C. today is independent of the states.

WHAT DOES THE TEMPLE LOOK LIKE?

Again, as with the tabernacle, we learn that God not only chose the site of the temple, but also gave the plans for its building. Indeed, even though David was not permitted to build the temple, God gave him the plans. Thus, in 1 Chronicles 28:19, we hear David say to Solomon: "Every part of this plan . . . was given to me in writing from the hand of the LORD."

The temple was a magnificent, ornate, and luxurious building, befitting its role as the house of God. By modern standards its dimensions were not overwhelming. According to its description in 1 Kings 6, it was ninety feet long and thirty feet wide, thus having a total interior of twenty-seven hundred square feet—again, not a gigantic building. Its height too was not excessive, being forty-five feet.

While the temple was not large, the quality of its workmanship was unsurpassed in ancient Israel. It was made of the finest woods and metals; in contrast with the tabernacle, no cloth materials are mentioned in its construction.

The building was divided into two parts by a partition that separated the back area—a third of the total area—from the rest of the interior. The back was where the ark of the covenant was kept, and its dimensions are given in 1 Kings 6:20 as "30 feet long, 30 feet wide, and 30 feet high"—a cube. This room was the most magnificent part of the temple compound, as we would expect since it housed the ark. Its ceiling and its walls, as well as its floors, were made of precious cedar wood covered with pure gold.

Moving out from this room, called the Most Holy Place, to the front two-thirds of the interior of the temple proper, we find a room thirty feet by sixty feet, thus 1800 square feet. Though not to the same extent, it too was luxuriously appointed. Its walls were cedar paneling, and its floor was cypress. While only the floor was covered with gold, its walls were carved with cherubim, palm trees, and open flowers, the significance of which we will discuss below.

Stepping out of the temple sanctuary, one would see two free-standing pillars. These were twenty-seven feet tall and eighteen feet in circumference, made of bronze. On top of the pillars were bronze capitals that were themselves seven and a half feet tall, decorated with floral motifs. Each had two hundred pomegranate shapes worked into it and the whole was shaped like a lily. The names of the pillars were Jakin and Boaz.

Also in the courtyard outside of the temple proper was a huge basin of water, resting on a base of twelve bronze oxen. This basin was fifteen feet across from rim to rim, seven and a half feet deep, and about forty-five feet in circumference. Its name was the Sea.

On three sides of the temple were a complex of rooms, perhaps for administration and storage (1 Kings

6:5–6). This completes our description of the physical dimensions of the temple.

The building project was begun in the fourth year of King Solomon's reign (966 B.C.). Though tens of thousands of laborers were involved in the work, it took seven years to complete. That much time was necessary even though we learn from 1 Chronicles 22–27 that Solomon's father, David, invested great effort and expense to prepare the materials for its construction. Still, additional materials were needed as the project developed. Solomon contacted the king of Tyre, Hiram, and worked out an arrangement with him to get even more of the precious cedar of Lebanon (1 Kings 5). The other materials needed were cypress wood, stone, bronze, and much gold.

THE SIGNIFICANCE OF TEMPLE SYMBOLISM

Like the tabernacle, the temple symbolized God's presence with his people. Accordingly, we again find heavenly imagery, such as the cherubim in the Holy of Holies, and garden imagery, connoting Eden, inside and out. We can also observe an intensification of precious materials, such as pure gold, as we move toward the specific place where God was thought to have his throne.

In addition, however, we find innovations as we compare the temple and the tabernacle. Interestingly, the innovations all point in the same direction. They point to the transition to a new era in the relationship between God and his people—that is, their establishment in the land. In this way, the innovations support what we have already seen in terms of the timing of the building of the temple.

In the first place, the temple, quite simply, was a permanent house, whereas the tabernacle was a portable tent. This important yet simple architectural feature indicates the transition from a wandering people to an established kingdom. The pillars enhanced this understanding of the symbolism of the temple. Pillars not only made a structure grander; they also imparted the impression of permanence. The names, Jakin and Boaz ("He has established" and "By his strength") encouraged this understanding.

Finally, the name of the basin of water, the Sea, has obvious significance. Throughout the Bible, the personified sea is often perceived as God's rival, representing the anti-creation forces of chaos. God fights the sea and controls its dangerous power. This image goes deep in the psyche of the ancient Near East and is found in Canaanite as well as Mesopotamian creation texts. Here, the Sea is bounded, controlled right outside the temple, which represents God's throne. This seems to represent the fact that God has defeated his adversaries, the former inhabitants of the land, and has firmly established his people there.

FOR FURTHER REFLECTION

1. Describe the differences in architectural detail between the tabernacle and the temple.
2. Why was David rejected as the builder of the temple?
3. We saw that the temple was built according to God's timing. Can we discern God's timing today? If so, to what extent and how?
4. Should our church architecture express our understanding of who God is and our relationship with him? If so, what form should our church architecture take?
5. We have seen that there are reasons for why the temple was located where it was in Jerusalem. What factors are appropriate to take into consideration concerning where we locate a church building.

5

THE FURNITURE OF THE
SANCTUARY: AN INSIDE LOOK
AT SACRED SPACE

❖

Having examined the structure of the tabernacle and the temple, we now take a look inside.[1] The sanctuary was not empty of furniture. The book of Exodus describes the items that filled the tent, and that is where we will center our discussion. The temple may not have held the identical items found in the tabernacle, but they were similar. Space and interest will not permit us to look at every piece of furniture in God's house, but we will look at the ark of the covenant, the menorah, the incense altar, the table that held the bread of presence, and the sacrificial altar. These are the pieces of furniture described in the book of Exodus.

THE ARK OF THE COVENANT

Described in Exodus 25:10–22, the ark was constructed from a rather simple design. It was a relatively small box, three and three-quarters feet long, two and a quarter feet wide, and two and a quarter feet high. It also had rings attached to the sides, through which poles were slid for carrying it.

While the design was simple, the composition of the ark was not. The poles and the box were made of precious acacia wood, and both were covered with gold. Indeed, the box was covered with gold both inside and outside. Furthermore, the cover was given a separate, special description and is said to have been made of pure gold. It is also said to have been the place where atonement took place. We will see the particular function of the cover below. At each side of the ark were to be placed gold statues of cherubim. The cherubim were especially powerful spiritual beings who served as protectors of God's holiness. They were at the sides of the ark with their heads bowed and their wings outstretched and touching each other.

The reason for their posture was that the ark was the most potent symbol of God's presence in the tabernacle. Indeed, it was seen as the footstool of his throne (1 Chron. 28:2), perhaps even occasionally as the throne itself (Jer. 3:16–17). God the King sat in his earthly house on his throne, and the cherubim, whose wings supported him, looked to the ground to shield their gaze from the radiance of his glory.

The ark was also a container. In Exodus 25 it is specifically mentioned as the place where the stone tablets of the covenant were held. Indeed, the presence of these tablets is surely the reason why one of the most common names of the ark is the "ark of the covenant." Recent research has shown that the conceptual world behind the Old Testament concept of covenant was a treaty between two nations, represented by their kings. In a typical treaty, two copies were made and each was deposited in the main sanctuary of its respective king's god. In the case of the covenant between God and his people Israel, there was, of course, only one God, and both copies were deposited in the one sanctuary, as our present text informs us—in the ark. At the heart of the covenant idea is the fact that God promised to be with his people. Thus, the ark was connected to the covenant as a concrete token of the divine presence.

The ark also played an important role in the battles of Israel. As a moveable symbol of God's presence, it was taken to the battlefield to signify God's support of the army. Indeed, this function of the ark is attested even during the wilderness wandering period. We have earlier seen that the wilderness wanderings were conceived as a long march into battle, and we noted the role of the ark at that point. Here, let me reiterate the point by quoting the language Moses used at the onset of a day's march. He would proclaim, "Arise, O LORD, and let your enemies be scattered! Let them flee before you!" (Num. 10:35).

It is not surprising that later when the people of Israel crossed the Jordan River for the first time into the promised land, the ark went first. The ark preceded the people by half a mile, and when it reached the Jordan, the waters of that river stopped flowing so that the people crossed over on dry ground. This miracle reminded the second generation, who were not present at the beginning of the wilderness wanderings, of the crossing of the Red Sea. It showed them that the same divine warrior who had defeated the Egyptians at that time was with them now as they faced the Canaanite foe (Josh. 3).

The first battle of the conquest took place at the formidable city of Jericho. The most ancient Palestinian city, Jericho had walls of renown. God instructed Joshua to march, with the ark, around Jericho once a day for six days. Then on the seventh day the Israelites were to march around the walls seven times and then blow their horns. The result was the collapse of the walls and the total defeat of this great city. Again, the pivotal role of the ark in this strategy is explained by the fact that it represented the presence of God with his people. God won the battle.

Psalm 24 is an interesting poem in this regard. The latter half of the song contains a dialogue, most naturally explained as taking place between the gatekeeper of Jerusalem and the priests, who has accompanied the army with the ark, now seeking entry back into the holy city.

The army priests begin by asking the gatekeepers to open the city to the army.

> Open up, ancient gates!
>   Open up, ancient doors,
>   and let the King of glory enter. (v. 7)

The gatekeepers know very well who the King of glory is, but their response allows the priests to celebrate God's attributes. They say,

> Who is the King of glory? (v. 8a)

The priests respond,

> The LORD, strong and mighty,
>   the LORD, invincible in battle. (v. 8b)

At that point, we are to presume that the gates open and amidst much celebration the ark is returned to its place in the Holy of Holies.

However, we must not think of the ark as a kind of magical box that could be manipulated at will. It was not a way to force God to use his power on behalf of his people. The story of Hophni and Phinehas proves this (1 Sam. 4). Hophni and Phinehas were the evil sons of the incompetent high priest Eli. They slept with the women who worked at the tabernacle, and they stole the sacrifices that were dedicated to God. They were also the leaders of the Israelite army, which was engaged in a conflict with the Philistines.

In the first battle, the Israelites had been soundly defeated by the Philistines. So Hophni and Phinehas, suddenly opting for a religious approach, said, "Let's bring the Ark of the Covenant of the LORD from Shiloh. If we carry it into battle with us, it will save us from our enemies" (1 Sam. 4:3). But they clearly had no faith in the God who was symbolically represented by the ark. They treated the ark rather as a magical box. So even with the presence of the ark on the battlefield, the Israelites were again defeated. Worse still, the ark was captured by the Philistines, who carted it off and placed it in the temple of their chief god, Dagon. In the meantime, messengers came to Eli and reported the army's defeat, as well as the loss of the ark. On hearing the news, he fell off his stoop, broke his neck, and died. His daughter-in-law went into labor, and when the child was born, he received the name Ichabod, "No Glory." After all, the glory of Israel, Yahweh represented by the ark, was now gone and in the enemy's possession.

The next scene is also instructive (1 Sam. 5). As mentioned, the Philistines had taken the ark and placed it before Dagon. In good ancient Near Eastern fashion, they felt that their god had shown his superiority over the god of the Israelites. The next morning, however, they came to the temple and saw Dagon collapsed before the ark. After hoisting him up, they returned the following morning to witness the same scene, though this time Dagon's head and hands were broken off.

This time the Philistines wisely sent the ark back to Israel. Indeed, they did so with great circumspection. They knew that the ark represented the presence of a God with whom they should not tamper. So they placed the ark on a cart that had never been used for a common task, hitched the cart to two cows, and set them free. The cows had given birth to calves, which had been penned up, perhaps as a last test of whether God was really behind the events taking place in Philistia. Cows naturally go to their calves, but when these cows were released, they wandered instead to Israel. This action, again, proves that God was intent on leaving Philistia.

Upon returning to Israel, the cart moved to the city of Beth-shemesh, near the Philistine-Israel border. However, the people of Beth-shemesh did not treat the ark with respect. Seventy people looked into it and thus were killed. The ark was moved to another city, Kiriath-jearim, where it stayed for twenty years.

The next phase in the history of the ark took place when David ascended the throne, captured Jerusalem, and proclaimed it his capital. In 2 Samuel 6 we read about the time he brought the ark from Kiriath-jearim to Jerusalem with great pomp and circumstance. This move was not accomplished without incident. On the way, the ark began to tip over and a man named Uzzah reacted in a way we might consider natural—he reached out to steady the ark. However, God did not see it that way and struck him dead immediately.

The text leaves God's motives unstated, but we might suggest that the Israelites had not shown the proper respect for the ark to allow it to be in a position where it might spill over. In any case, this incident put the "fear of God" in David, who let the ark sit in the city of Gath for three months while he decided what to do. In those three months, the home of Obed-edom, where the ark was kept, flourished, indicating to David the potential for blessing in Jerusalem. He accordingly gave orders and brought the ark to Jerusalem. He was so happy that he danced with joy (and little clothing) in front of the ark as it made its way into the city.

As we have already seen, it was not God's will that David build the temple, but rather his son, Solomon. Once the temple was built, the priests carried the ark into the Holy of Holies (1 Kings 8:6–8).

We presume that the ark resided in the Holy of Holies for many years. However, the biblical text rarely mentions the ark after this time. This raises important questions in our minds that can be very difficult, if not impossible, to answer. Was the ark still in existence? Our answer must be yes if we take 2 Chronicles 35:3 seriously. This is the sole reference to the ark in a historical book after the time of Solomon. Much about this reference is debated. What is clear is that the ark existed at the time of Josiah (640–609 B.C.). Some scholars, it is true, deny the historical veracity of the reference in Chronicles and argue that the ark had been destroyed as early as the raid of Shishak, the Egyptian pharaoh, during the reign of Rehoboam, Solomon's son. However, such an act is not mentioned in the Bible; it is only implied in that the ark is not mentioned, except in this late reference in 2 Chronicles, after the time of Solomon. Other scholars[2] believe that the ark was removed and destroyed by King Manasseh, who ruled just before Josiah.

While we take the reference in 2 Chronicles 35 seriously, we admit that the ultimate fate of the ark is shrouded in mystery. Its end is never mentioned. Of course, this leads to fanciful attempts to describe where it ended up—all the way down to Steven Spielberg's movie *Raiders of the Lost Ark*!

Before leaving the subject of the ark, we want to mention specifically the lid of the ark, which is given the provocative title of "mercy seat." This was the place where God said he would meet with Moses. Furthermore, as the name itself suggests, and as Leviticus 16:2, 13–15 states, "It conveys notions of forgiveness and of protection from the power of sin."[3]

THE MENORAH

The tabernacle was covered with four thick curtains. No light would have seeped through, except at the opening, and only if the entrance curtain was pulled back. Thus, it is not surprising, from a purely functional point of view, that God directed Moses to construct a lamp to illuminate the interior. The divine directions for building it are found in Exodus 25:31–40:

Make a lampstand of pure, hammered gold. The entire lampstand and its decorations will be one piece—the base, center stem, lamp cups, buds, and blossoms. It will have six branches, three branches going out from each side of the center stem. Each of the six branches will hold a cup shaped like an almond blossom, complete with buds and petals. The center stem of the lampstand will be decorated with four almond blossoms, complete with buds and petals. One blossom will be set beneath each pair of branches where they extend from the center stem. The decorations and branches must all be one piece with the stem, and they must be hammered from pure gold. Then make the seven lamps for the lampstand, and set them so they reflect their light forward. The lamp snuffers and trays must also be made of pure gold. You will need seventy-five pounds of pure gold for the lampstand and its accessories.

Be sure that you make everything according to the pattern I have shown you here on the mountain.

The lamp is hard to picture in detail from this description. Later visual representation—like that on the victory arch of Titus showing the Roman theft of the menorah after the destruction of the temple in A.D. 70—shows a candlestick with a central shaft with three additional candles on each side. However, we cannot be certain that this was the form of the original menorah described in Exodus. Indeed, Numbers 8 informs us that Aaron placed the lamp so that the light went forward, which seems odd on the basis of the usual depiction of the menorah. Furthermore, if (and this is a big "if") the lampstand in Zechariah 4 reflects the tabernacle/temple menorah, then it also disabuses us of the traditional picture of it. It may have been more like a basin, filled with oil, with wicks laid in depressions made in the rim. In any case, we know that the menorah was large because it took a whole talent of gold (seventy-five pounds) to make it!

However, we are much more interested in its symbolic significance than its physical appearance. From the time of Josephus down to the present day, some have tried to associate the number seven with the number of planets known at the time.[4] Perhaps there is some truth to this speculation, but that is what it is—speculation.

We are on much firmer textual ground if we recognize the menorah as a tree. The tree-like qualities of the menorah were much more than decoration. In chapter 2 we noted the association of trees with places of worship. A tree-like menorah reminds us of the garden of Eden and so represents the presence of God on earth. Heavenly and Edenic imagery thus permeated the tabernacle. Furthermore, this tree was on fire. We are perhaps to associate this with another episode where God made his presence known on earth, namely the burning bush (Exod. 3).

Some interpreters have made much of the symbolism of light here. However, that theme—as opposed to the symbolism of fire—does not appear often, if at all, in the Old Testament.

According to Leviticus 24:1–4, the menorah was to be kept lit all the time. This would serve as a reminder that God made his presence known in the tabernacle precincts just as he did throughout Eden, which itself represented heaven.

THE INCENSE ALTAR

A second altar in the tabernacle is mentioned in Exodus 30:1–10. This altar had the same basic shape, including horns, as the altar of burnt offerings, but was much smaller. Its dimensions were eighteen inches wide and long, and three feet high. It too was built out of acacia wood and was covered, but with pure gold rather than bronze. That difference reflects the proximity to the Holy of Holies, since the incense altar was placed "just outside the inner curtain, opposite the Ark's cover—the place of atonement—that rests on the Ark of the Covenant" (v. 6). This description suggests that the altar of incense was on an axis with the bronze altar in the courtyard at the entrance to the Holy Place. The incense altar stood at the entrance between the Holy Place and the Holy of Holies. The third and climactic part of this axis was the ark of the covenant itself.[5]

A special formula was used to make the incense that would be burned on this altar (Exod. 30:34–38). Its sacral character was indicated by the prohibition of its use outside of the tabernacle.

The altar of incense had one very practical purpose. With all the slaughtering of sacrifices and the manipulation of blood, the odor would have been overpowering without incense. The sweet smell of incense was pleasing to the Lord, and twice a day the priests were to light the incense burners. The altar itself would have been associated with the presence of God by means of its close association with the ark and the tabernacle.

THE TABLE OF THE BREAD OF PRESENCE

Exodus 25:23–30 describes the construction of a table three feet long, one and a half feet wide, and two and a quarter feet high. It was made of acacia wood and covered with pure gold. What is most interesting about this table is that on it was to be placed the bread of the presence. Leviticus 24:5–9 describes the bread and the ritual associated with it. The day before the Sabbath the priests were to bake loaves for placing on the table the next day.

The old loaves from the previous Sabbath were to be eaten by the priests, not discarded, since the loaves were dedicated to such a holy use. Leviticus 24:8 tells us that this bread was important because it was "a continual part of the covenant."

The very name of the bread, "presence," indicates that it represented the presence of God with his people. The twelve loaves certainly represented the twelve tribes. The covenant designated the relationship that bound Israel and God together. Covenants were often sealed with a meal, and a host of passages in Deuteronomy talk about Israel or its leaders eating in the presence of the Lord. Thus, the loaves were a reminder of the intimate relationship the people of God enjoyed with their covenant Lord.

THE SACRIFICIAL ALTAR

We conclude our study of the furniture of the tabernacle with a look at an object constructed not for the interior but for the exterior. Just in front of the tabernacle, but within the courtyard area (Exod. 27:1–8), Moses was to build an altar out of acacia wood that was seven and a half feet square and four and a half feet high. This altar was covered with bronze and is described as having horns on its upper corners. The altar was for the purpose of offering burnt sacrifices, so all sorts of accessories (ash buckets, shovels, basins, meat hooks, and firepans) were also to be made out of bronze.

The altar was made of bronze, rather than gold, because it was located outside the tent. The principle we have seen is that though everything in the entire tabernacle precinct was holy and important, the closer an object was to the Holy of Holies, the more sacred it was, a fact highlighted by the expense of the material out of which it was made.

Of course, the original altar of the tabernacle has not

survived to the present day, but other comparable examples have been uncovered by archeological research. One example, found in the archeological site associated with biblical Arad, has the same features. The "horns" are rounded projections on each of the corners of the top of the altar. They were built of one piece with the body of the altar; they were not added separately. The function of the horns is best thought of as allowing the priest to tie the sacrifice down on top.

The biblical text is explicit about the fact that the blood of the sacrifice, especially the sin offering (Lev. 4:18, 25, 30, 34),[6] was to be smeared on the horns of the altar before the animal was burned[7] (Exod. 29:12). Symbolically, the horns may well have represented God's strength. It is well known that horns used in noncultic contexts referred to one's strength, so here the horns represented the strength of God. This may also explain why those seeking asylum from vengeance grabbed the horns of the altar (1 Kings 1:50–51; 2:28–29; Exod. 21:13–14). This also helps explain why judgment against idols, whose altars also had horns, was expressed in Amos by cutting the horns (3:14).

The altar was extremely important because sacrifice was extremely important. Since the Fall, no human being could approach the intimate presence of God without offering a sacrifice of an animal, whose death would substitute for the death of the worshiper. Accordingly, as we have seen, altars were a part of the worship of the people of God since the Fall. The placement of the altar outside of the tabernacle proper signified that sinners had to offer sacrifice before getting closer to the awesome presence of their Lord.

The ark of the covenant, the lampstand, the table of the bread of presence, the sacrificial altar, and the incense altar constituted the furniture of God's house in the tabernacle area. Each of these items also found a place in Solomon's temple. Each had its distinctive function within the complex, as well as unique symbolic significance. However, in its own special way, each also had one fundamental truth—it pointed to the presence of a holy God in the midst of a sinful people.

FOR FURTHER REFLECTION

1. Some modern church buildings are plain and others are ornate. Why the difference? Which do you prefer? Is there a theological rationale for one or the other?
2. Read Jeremiah 7. At the time of Jeremiah people had taken the view that God lived in Jerusalem and would allow nothing to happen to Jerusalem under any circumstance. Criticize their view from what we know about temple theology.
3. Some modern churches burn incense, as they did in the Old Testament temple. Should this practice be allowed? Why or why not?
4. We have seen the ways God manifested his presence in the tabernacle/temple. How does God manifest his presence in your life? At your church?
5. We have seen that the menorah is a tree symbol. Where else in the Bible is the tree used as a symbol of divine presence?

6

THE COMING OF IMMANUEL:
WHERE DO CHRISTIANS
FIND HOLY SPACE?

⁘

Where do *we* go to be in the presence of God? God's people are those who desire to be with God. The psalmist well expresses this yearning:

> As the deer pants for streams of water,
>   so I long for you, O God.
> I thirst for God, the living God.
>   When can I come and stand before him?
>   (Ps. 42:1–2)

In the Old Testament, God chose specific locations where he made his presence known. These areas, which we can collectively call sanctuaries, were surrounded by prohibitions since a holy God does not tolerate the presence of sin. Another psalm gives voice to this truth:

> Who may worship in your sanctuary, LORD?
>   Who may enter your presence on your holy
>   hill?
> Those who lead blameless lives

and do what is right,
   speaking the truth from sincere hearts.
Those who refuse to slander others
   or harm their neighbors
   or speak evil of their friends.
         (Ps. 15:1–3)

Psalm 15 goes on to enumerate even more conditions imposed on those who desire to be in the presence of God. Even this partial list evokes the cry, "Who, then, can be in the presence of God?" Indeed, in part two we will detail the role that sacrifice plays in providing access to God in the sanctuary. But still, as we read the Old Testament, we cannot escape the tension between the desire to be in God's presence and the difficulty of coming near him. One feels the joy, but also the yearning induced by distance, of the psalmist when he says,

How lovely is your dwelling place,
   O LORD Almighty.
I long, yes, I faint with longing
   to enter the courts of the LORD.
With my whole being, body and soul,
   I will shout joyfully to the living God.
. . . .
A single day in your courts
   is better than a thousand anywhere else!
I would rather be a gatekeeper in the house of
     my God
   than live the good life in the homes of the
     wicked. (Ps. 84:1–2, 10)

How amazing, then, it is when we read about the coming of our Immanuel ("God with us"). In the New Testament, we learn that it is Jesus who is our tabernacle/temple.

JESUS, OUR "SACRED SPACE," ACCORDING TO THE GOSPELS

The opening of John's gospel is reminiscent of the start of Genesis. "In the beginning" was the Word of God, who was God himself. The startling truth of the good news is that this Word "became human and lived here on earth among us" (John 1:14). The New Living Translation, here quoted, like all other modern translations, obscures an important point captured by a more literal rendition: the Word "became flesh and tabernacled among us." What John has done is to take the Greek word for tabernacle (*skēnē*) and make a verb out of it (*skēnoō*). While this verbal idea is admittedly difficult to communicate in contemporary English, it presents a powerful image with deep roots in the Old Testament. Jesus is the tabernacle. Where he is, there is God. When someone met Jesus, he or she was in the presence of God.

During his lifetime, Jesus showed great respect for the temple that was standing in Jerusalem. It was the second temple, built after the Babylonian captivity, but expanded to a new glory by Herod the Great. When Jesus was just twelve years old, he went to the temple with his parents, but did not leave with them, remaining instead to discuss profundities with the religious teachers there. When his frightened parents hurried back to retrieve him, Jesus responded, "You should have known that I would be in my Father's house" (Luke 2:49). Jesus recognized the special importance of the temple even in his day; it was where one went to be with God.

That is why he could not tolerate the disrespect and exploitation of the moneychangers (John 2:13–25). They were using the temple for their own financial gain. The disciples, we hear, thought of Psalm 69:9 as they watched Christ forcibly remove the moneychangers: "Passion for God's house burns within me" (John 2:17). According to Jesus, they were turning God's house into a market.

But even at the moment that he showed such concern for the sanctity of the temple, Jesus intimated that a new reality was on the horizon. As the religious leaders confronted Jesus concerning his authority over the temple, they demanded a sign and he responded: "All right. . . . Destroy this temple and in three days I will raise it up" (John 2:19). The leaders were dumbfounded; how could Jesus build a temple in three days when it took years to build it in the first place? Though he apparently did not make this public at the time, the disciples, whose later post-resurrection perspective is revealed in the gospel of John, ultimately recognized that he was talking about his body. Jesus was making a profound and subtle connection between the temple and himself.

Although Jesus respected the temple, he knew it was temporary. It was a shadow that would disappear when the light of the reality arrived. The account of his conversation with the Samaritan woman at the well articulates this clearly while also expressing the consequences for worship.

The woman Jesus encounters at the well is not given a name, but rather is identified by her location—the woman of Samaria. In the first century A.D. and before, the Samaritans were thought of as ethnically hybrid and religiously suspect. That Jesus would talk to a Samaritan, and a woman at that, is nearly scandalous. But he does, for the purpose of telling her where to find true satisfaction in life.

Our interest in this conversation is much narrower, however. It centers on the question that has preoccupied us through several chapters. The woman, recognizing Jesus as an authority, asks the same question, "So tell me, why is it that you Jews insist that Jerusalem is the only place of worship, while we Samaritans claim it is here at Mount Gerizim, where our ancestors worshiped?" (John 4:20).

The controversy behind this question had separated

Samaritans from Jewish worshipers of God for many years. Its origins are shrouded in mystery, but it may go all the way back to when the Assyrians deported a large portion of the ten northern tribes away from their homeland. These exiles were never again heard from, but some of the original inhabitants were still in the land. In keeping with the Assyrian policy of ousting conquered people from their homelands, the Assyrians soon replaced the original inhabitants. The new settlers were not previously worshipers of Yahweh, but they likely intermarried with some of the original inhabitants and became at least hybrid worshipers of Yahweh. After all, many Near Eastern people had what might be called a landlocked view of their gods. There were many gods, and they all had their bit of real estate. So we can imagine how these new inhabitants of the northern kingdom (Samaria) may have easily absorbed this new worship.

A little later the Babylonians defeated the southern kingdom, Judah, and likewise deported a portion of the people to Babylon. It does not appear, however, that the Babylonians deported other people to Judah, though again some of the original inhabitants of Judah never left. The temple had been destroyed in 586 B.C., so when the returnees entered the land again, they had no place to worship. They quickly built the altar so that they could resume sacrificial worship (Ezra 3), and also started the reconstruction of the temple proper.

While they were rebuilding the temple, some people described as "enemies of Judah and Benjamin" approached the leaders and said, "Let us build with you, for we worship your God just as you do. We have sacrificed to him every since King Esarhaddon of Assyria brought us here" (Ezra 4:1–2). In response to this, though, Zerubbabel and the other leaders absolutely forbade their participation. This, of course, displeased those who had offered help, and so they turned around and tried to obstruct the temple rebuilding.

These events may be the roots of the division that led to worship on two mountains—Gerizim in the north near the city of Shechem, and Mount Sinai in the south in Jerusalem. It was, at heart, a dispute over where God made his presence known.

In answer to the Samaritan woman's question, Jesus leaves no doubt over who worships God rightly. It was the Jewish people who followed God's instructions as presented in the books of Samuel-Kings to build the temple on Mount Sinai.[1] Furthermore, he uses her question as the occasion to announce the next great development in appropriate worship:

> The time is coming and is already here when true worshipers will worship the Father in spirit and in truth. The Father is looking for anyone who will worship him that way. For God is Spirit, so those who worship him must worship in spirit and in truth. (John 4:23–24)

This worship, Jesus explains, is more in keeping with the nature of God, since God himself is a spirit.

What a radical idea from a first-century Palestinian Jewish teacher like Jesus. But that is the point: Jesus is more than a teacher as he reveals to his disciples an additional teaching about the temple.

One day Jesus and his disciples were in the temple and the disciples were marveling over the magnificence of the temple. The stones of Herod's temple were massive, suggesting permanence and grandeur. Jesus, though, turned to them and undermined the disciples' understanding of the temple by saying, "Not one stone here will be left on another; every one will be thrown down" (Mark 13:2 NIV). We have already seen that Jesus hinted at this when he drove the moneychangers out of the temple, but there he added the idea that he would rebuild the temple in three days. In fact, soon thereafter Jesus found himself standing before Caiaphas, the high priest, as others accused him of saying "I will destroy this man-made temple and in three days will build another, not made by man" (Mark 14:58 NIV).

Of course, the three days alerts us to Christ's meaning here. He was anticipating that after three days, he would be raised from the dead. In short, Jesus identified himself as the temple. Why is the temple no longer necessary? Because we have Jesus, who is God himself.

Of course, not everyone can be in the physical presence of Jesus, and certainly not after his death and resurrection. That is true of the man Jesus, but we must remember that after Jesus was raised and was seated at the right hand of the Father, he sent the Holy Spirit to us. In a way that Paul would later explicate (see below), the Holy Spirit's presence with us means that we are constantly in the presence of God.

And, wonder of wonders, when Jesus died, there was an immediate visible sign that a transformation took place. According to Matthew 27:51, at the moment of Jesus' death "the curtain of the Temple was torn in two, from top to bottom." This is surely a reference to the curtain that separated the Holy Place from the Holy of Holies. No longer is there a division between secular and sacred, profane and holy. Everywhere is imbued with the presence of God. In this way, we find ourselves nudging toward Eden.

JESUS, OUR "SACRED SPACE," ACCORDING TO THE EPISTLES

As we turn to the letters of the New Testament, we find that the presentation of Jesus as the fulfillment of the temple continues, but with new and important twists. A number of intensely interesting passages are related to this theme. We will begin by looking at the teaching of the book of Hebrews.

Hebrews was clearly addressed to a Jewish audience.[2] We can infer this from the pervasiveness of Old Testament references in the book. Some scholars try to pinpoint a specific group within first-century Judaism based on the topics the anonymous author addresses, but this detail is unimportant for our study.

We will have recourse to the book of Hebrews in all four parts of this volume, since it is the contention of the author of Hebrews that Jesus fulfilled all the ceremonial law. Jesus is the ultimate priest, the ultimate sacrifice, and the ultimate festival. Indeed the teaching of Hebrews on the tabernacle/temple is situated in the discussion of Christ as priest and sacrifice. Jesus ministers as priest and brings himself as the once-and-for-all sacrifice in "the true place of worship that was built by the Lord and not by human hands" (Heb. 8:2). This true place of worship is heaven itself. Jesus our High Priest has entered heaven and sits at God's right hand. In comparison with the Old Testament priests, who, according to Hebrews 8:5, "serve in a place of worship that is only a copy, a shadow of the real one in heaven," Jesus presents his sacrifice in the real, heavenly temple. This point is re-emphasized in Hebrews 9:1–10, where the author further describes the old earthly tabernacle. Its importance and significance have faded away as Jesus has entered the true Holy Place in heaven.

The message of Hebrews, in short, relates to our study in this way: Because of Jesus' presence, the importance of the sanctuary—altar, tabernacle, temple—has fallen away.

Paul takes this truth in a new and surprising direction. Though he does not teach this directly, he certainly understands that Jesus claimed to be the fulfillment of the tabernacle/temple. To Paul, this has great implications for us as Christians, beyond the fact that Christians no longer have a temple-based religion. Indeed, it means that Christians themselves are corporately and individually temples. This teaching is developed with a variety of nuances.

In Ephesians 2:19–22, we read,

> So now you Gentiles are no longer strangers and foreigners. You are citizens along with all of God's holy people. You are members of God's family. We are his house, built on the foundation of the apostles and the prophets. And the cornerstone is Christ Jesus himself. We who believe are carefully joined together, becoming a holy temple for the Lord. Through him you Gentiles are also joined together as part of this dwelling where God lives by his Spirit.

The picture is powerful. Christians are the stones of God's house. The teaching of the apostles and prophets, the Scriptures, is the foundation on which this house rests. But of course the most important stone, the stone without which the structure does not stand, is Jesus himself. The last sentence tells us why gentile believers, and by implication all believers, are part of the temple. Namely, God lives in us in the person of the Holy Spirit. We are filled with the Spirit at our conversion, just as the tabernacle/temple was filled with the presence of God.

This truth is applied in an ethical direction in a number of places, for example 2 Corinthians 6:14–16:

> Don't team up with those who are unbelievers. How can goodness be a partner with wickedness? How can light live with darkness? What harmony can there be between Christ and the Devil? How can a believer be a partner with an unbeliever? And what union can there be between God's temple and idols? For we are the temple of the living God.

Paul here teaches that Christians are filled with the Spirit and are therefore like the temple in Jerusalem. In striking contrast, unbelievers are temples too, and like the pagan temples of the gods who rivaled Yahweh, they too are filled—but with the presence of false gods, here called "idols." Paul tells the Corinthians that the two cannot be mixed, and believers should avoid intimacies with unbelievers.

Elsewhere he applies this principle in a sexual direction, in 1 Corinthians 6:18–20:

> Run away from sexual sin! No other sin so clearly affects the body as this one does. For sexual immorality is a sin against your own body. Or don't you know that your body is the temple of the Holy Spirit, who lives in you and was given to you by God? You do not belong to yourself, for God bought you with a high price. So you must honor God with your body.

How can this be? How can Jesus and his followers both be temples? Part of the answer might be in the flexibility of metaphor. But a large part of the answer, I believe, is found in Paul's presentation of our union with Christ. We find our identity now in Christ. He stands in our place before God.

THE ESCHATOLOGICAL TEMPLE: SACRED SPACE IN THE END

The final two chapters of the book of Revelation present us with a glimpse of heaven. The imagery is exciting and suggestive, but also enigmatic. As with metaphor generally, it both reveals the truth and conceals it. We come away knowing something wonderful is in store for God's people, though we really have little by way of concrete description.

Part of the imagery of heaven continues, indeed culminates, the theme we have been tracing in this section. Heaven is pictured as a "New Jerusalem," so the question is immediately raised: Does it have a temple like the old Jerusalem? After all, that was really what made the city of Jerusalem so important; it was where God chose to make his special presence known on earth.

Revelation 21:22 leaves us in no doubt. The New Jerusalem, that is heaven, will have no temple at all: "No temple could be seen in the city, for the Lord God Almighty and the Lamb are its temple." The reason for the lack of a temple makes it all clear. When Christ has come again and has punished all sin, there is no need for a temple. The temple represented heaven on earth; now the people of God live in the reality of heaven. The temple symbolized Eden and the original harmony that existed between God and his human subjects. Eden has been restored, and as a matter of fact something greater than Eden. Revelation 22:1–2 expresses this thought clearly:

> And the angel showed me a pure river with the water of life, clear as crystal, flowing from the throne of God and of the Lamb, coursing down the center of the main street. On each side of the river grew a tree of life, bearing twelve crops of fruit, with a fresh crop each month. The leaves were used for medicine to heal the nations.

FOR FURTHER REFLECTION

1. What does it mean that you are the temple? How should you act?
2. What does it mean that the church is the temple? What implications does this metaphor have for the church today?

3. Reflect on your desires, goals, and interests. Do you yearn to experience the presence of God? Why or why not?
4. Does the picture or glimpse of heaven we get in Revelation 21–22 excite you? Again, explore the reasons for your desire or lack of it.

PART TWO

SACRED ACTS

Certainly, there was more to worship in the Old Testament than sacrifice. Songs were sung, prayers were offered, the Word was read and reflected upon. However, we focus on sacrifice here for two reasons.

In the first place, it is the strangest aspect of Israel's worship to us living in the twenty-first century, and so it needs more explanation than do other Old Testament worship acts. Second, in an important sense, as we will see in the pages to follow, sacrifice was a crucial aspect to Old Testament worship. To worship God, people must be in his presence. But it is not easy to be in God's presence. Human beings are sinners, covenant breakers. God's holy judgment would break out against any sinner who dared to come into his presence. Sacrifice was the way that the Old Testament saints recognized and atoned for their sin as they came before the Lord.

Accordingly, much attention is given to sacrifice in the Old Testament. With that in mind, let's turn now to that topic to gain a deeper understanding of its role and function.

7

THE 'OLAH:
THE WHOLE BURNT
OFFERING

A t Sinai, God gave Moses instructions concerning the types of sacrifices he wanted his faithful people to offer him.[1] In Leviticus 1–7 we have the description of five different kinds of sacrifices, each with its own ritual, and all with different but often overlapping purposes. In the next three chapters, we will treat each of the five separately.[2]

It has often been conjectured that these seven chapters in Leviticus were written for the priests. They provide a kind of bare-bones description of the ritual without much hint of the significance or the symbolic value of the sacrifice. Not infrequently we can figure out the purpose of the sacrifice from its name, context, or use. However, it may be helpful to begin with an explanation of the three main functions of sacrifice in general. We will then show how each of the five sacrifices supports this understanding of purpose.

THE THREE FUNCTIONS OF SACRIFICE

Atonement

Atonement is arguably the most fundamental function of sacrifice. As we will see, certain individual sacrifices—such as the *minhah* sacrifice—made no atonement, but were likely always offered in conjunction with another sacrifice that did atone for sins.

"Atonement" is an English word contrived from the phrase "at-one-ment." It denotes making a unity, restoring a relationship. The idea behind it is that sin has created a break in the relationship between God and his human subjects. Sacrifice is an integral part of the ritual that reestablishes the unity between God and humans.

With this explanation, we can better understand the connection between covenant and sacrifice. After all, "covenant" is the leading metaphor for describing God's relationship to his people. It is a legal term similar to "treaty," and it comes with law as well as promise.[3] If one breaks God's law—that is, sins—he or she is alienated from God. The atoning function of sacrifice overcomes the obstacle that sin presents to one's relationship with God.

The Hebrew verb translated "atone" is *kipper,* the piel of the root *kapar.* A longstanding debate has swirled around the proper etymology of this Hebrew word. On the one hand, some scholars appeal to the Akkadian root, meaning "wipe off," while others say the historical origins of the Hebrew word are closer to the Arabic "cover" or "conceal." Much homiletical hay has been made out of these etymologies. When God atones for our sins, are our sins wiped away and no longer there, or are they covered over, there but not seen?

Practically speaking, it makes little difference to us, and methodologically speaking, it is dangerous to base our understanding of a word too much on its etymology rather than on its use. With that in mind, we simply say that the word means "atone" and involves our reconciliation with God after sin has broken the harmony of that relationship.

Gift

A second significance of a sacrifice is that it is a gift to God. As we will see below in particular with the *min-*

hah sacrifice, God is our King, and we as his subjects must bring him gifts. Of course, God does not need our gifts for his sustenance, but he does in some sense derive pleasure from receiving them from us.

Fellowship or Communion

Some sacrifices—note in particular the *shelamim* sacrifice—emphasize fellowship. This indicates in the first place a communion between God and the worshiper, but also between the worshipers generally and the priestly community in particular. This aspect of sacrifice is highlighted in that not all of the offering is devoted to God, but certain designated parts of the sacrifice can be eaten by the circle of worshipers.

So the three main functions or purposes of sacrifices are atonement, gift, and communion. With this understanding, we turn now to the first sacrifice described in the book of Leviticus, the *'olah* sacrifice, frequently translated as "whole burnt offering."

THE *'OLAH* SACRIFICE

The first sacrifice described in Leviticus (chap. 1; also 6:8–18) is the *'olah* sacrifice. By virtue of its coming first in the list, we can assume its importance, and that will be confirmed by our examination of its meaning. With the exception of the Day of Atonement, where the sin offering took center place, the *'olah* sacrifice was the most important sacrifice at Israelite festivals (Num. 28–29). Perhaps even more importantly, the *'olah* was offered twice each day, once in the morning and once in the evening (Num. 28:1–8).

But first, how should we translate the Hebrew term *'olah*? It is often translated "(whole) burnt offering" (NLT; NIV), and while this is a good description of the procedure of the sacrifice, it is not what the Hebrew term means. It actually means "rising up" and must refer to the smoke that rose from the altar during the ritual. The smoke rose from the earth into the heavens, where God pronounced it "very pleasing" (Lev. 1:9, 13, 17).

The Procedure of the 'olah Sacrifice

The procedure of the offering was quite complex, involving both the priest and the worshiper in a number of steps. First, the sacrificial offering was brought to the entrance of the tabernacle. At this point, the worshiper laid hands on the head of the animal. It is with this act that we get at the heart of the significance of the 'olah sacrifice: "So the LORD will accept it as your substitute, thus making atonement for you" (Lev. 1:4). Below we will expand on the idea of atonement in this sacrifice, but the hand-laying ritual was certainly to be understood as a mode of identification. It was not a magical transference between the one offering sacrifice and the animal, but rather a symbolic identification.

This step was crucial because when the animal was sacrificed, clearly the death of the animal occurred in place of the death of the worshiper. The assumption behind this was that the worshiper was a sinner coming into the presence of a holy Lord (v. 5). As a sinner, the human participant deserved death, but the animal stood in his or her place.

The worshiper then slaughtered the animal, the verb implying the slitting of the animal's throat. After the death of the animal, the blood was collected and sprinkled against the side of the altar. The priest performed this act. Indeed, anything having to do with the blood and the altar was the responsibility of the priest. The altar represented the presence of God, and the drained blood highlighted the death of the animal. The carcass of the animal was then carefully prepared as it was skinned and cut into pieces, and the internal organs were washed. Then the entire animal was placed on the altar by the priests and burned completely, the smoke rising to the Lord. Indeed, the chapter mentions that the sacrifice was "very pleasing to the LORD" (vv. 9, 13, 17).

According to Leviticus 6:8–13 the fire on the altar was to burn continually; it was never to be put out. The ashes were to be collected every morning and placed initially beside the altar, and then eventually carried off the grounds of the tabernacle to a place that was ceremonially clean.

The 'olah and Atonement

We have discussed the nature of atonement in relationship to all sacrifices in general. Here we will comment specifically on how the 'olah related to atonement.

That the 'olah had implications for atonement is explicit in Leviticus 1, particularly in verse 4, which reads, "Lay your hand on its head so the LORD will accept it as your substitute, thus making atonement for you." It is clear that the death of the animal represented the death of the sinner approaching the presence of God. It was the worshiper who deserved to die, but God accepted the animal as a substitute. This acknowledgment of sin and its consequences was the most important aspect of the 'olah sacrifice. That the entirety of the sacrifice (with the exception of the hide—7:8) was burned indicates that this sacrifice emphasized the importance of the atonement function at the expense of gift and fellowship.

Reading Leviticus 1 in the context of the whole Bible leads us to the understanding that the sacrifice did not automatically lead to atonement and the forgiveness of sins. Moreover, we wouldn't expect Leviticus 1, which is a priestly manual for sacrifice, to mention repentance. However, in other texts we clearly see that offering a sacrifice without the right attitude had absolutely no effect on the status of the worshiper before God. According to Micah 6:6–8,

> What can we bring to the LORD to make up for
> what we've done? Should we bow before God

with offerings of yearling calves? Should we offer him thousands of rams and tens of thousands of rivers of olive oil? Would that please the LORD? Should we sacrifice our firstborn children to pay for the sins of our souls? Would that make him glad? No, O people, the LORD has already told you what is good, and this is what he requires: to do what is right, to love mercy, and to walk humbly with your God.

This sentiment is expressed also by Hosea, as well as David:

> I want you to be merciful; I don't want your sacrifices. I want you to know God; that's more important than burnt offerings. (Hos. 6:6).

> You take no delight in sacrifices or offerings.
>   Now that you have made me listen, I finally understand—
> you don't require burnt offerings or sin offerings.
> Then I said, "Look, I have come.
>   And this has been written about me in your scroll:
> I take joy in doing your will, my God,
>   for your law is written on my heart."
>   (Ps. 40:6–8)

In this regard, sacrifice is similar to the sacraments of baptism and the Lord's Supper, outward signs of an inward reality. The procedure, particularly the blood manipulation, emphasizes this.

The Animal Used in the Ritual

The procedure we described above follows the ritual for the sacrifice of a bull for the 'olah. However, as the passage continues, we see that there were some alternatives given to the worshiper. Leviticus 1:10–13 describes the procedure for offering a sheep or goat, and 1:14–17 describes the sacrifice of a bird. These options reflect a flexibility based on the economic status of the one offering the sacrifice. If one could not afford a bull, then a goat or sheep would do.[4] But if even this was beyond the person's means, then a mere bird would suffice. Indeed, the psalmist indicates that it was not the cost of the gift but the motive that was important:

> Then I will praise God's name with singing,
>   and I will honor him with thanksgiving.
> For this will please the LORD more than sacrific-
>   ing an ox
>   or presenting a bull with its honors and
>   hooves.
> The humble will see their God at work and be
>   glad. (Ps. 69:30–32)

However, we are led to believe that if someone could afford a bull and showed up with a turtledove, that would not have been appreciated by the priest or God himself.

In the case of an animal from the herd or the flock, the text is explicit that the animal should have no physical defects (Lev. 1:3, 10). This qualification is missing with respect to birds, probably because they were the option for the poorest people, who likely trapped them. The prohibition of animals with some physical defect was, of course, to guard against the practice of bringing a worthless animal as a gift to the Lord.

Right from the beginning we can see godless individuals trying to get away with something less than the best. In Genesis 4, we see Cain and Abel bringing a sacrifice to the Lord,[5] with opposite results. It has often been asked why God rejected Cain's sacrifice and accepted Abel's. The key is likely to be found in the adjectives used in this account. While

Cain's sacrifice is described very plainly, Abel's lamb is described as "choice" and "the best of his flock" (Gen. 4:4).[6]

An argument can be made that the 'olah sacrifice is foundational to the sacrificial system. We have seen that it was offered daily as part of the set ritual of the sanctuary, as well as at every yearly festival, with the exception of the Day of Atonement. Furthermore, individuals would bring their own bull, sheep, lamb, goat, or bird for their own personal sacrifice. The prevalence of the 'olah should be connected to its primary function as an atonement for sin. Later, we will see that other sacrifices also had atonement value, but either that was a secondary theme of the sacrifice (shelamim), or the atonement was for a specific type of sin (hattat and asham). As we will point out in a later chapter, this central atoning significance of the 'olah would account for its important use in the New Testament.

FOR FURTHER REFLECTION

1. What was it about the 'olah that made it the foundational sacrifice?
2. What does "atonement" mean to you theologically and personally?
3. Why were there different sacrifices and not just one?
4. The 'olah was foundational to Old Testament worship. Is there anything so foundational in today's worship?

8

THE *MINHAH* AND *SHELAMIM*: TRIBUTE AND FELLOWSHIP OFFERINGS

⸙

The *minhah* and *shelamim* offerings are the second and third described in the ritual instructions of Leviticus.

THE *MINHAH* OFFERING

The *minhah* (Lev. 2; also 6:14–23) is often called the "grain offering," not because the Hebrew word *minhah* means grain, but because this sacrifice was composed of grain. As a grain offering, it was obviously not a sacrifice that involved the shedding of blood, and for that reason no atonement language is connected with it. As we will see below, the emphasis of the *minhah* was on giving a gift. However, due to the offensiveness of sin, human beings need atonement before approaching God with a gift, and so we are not surprised to observe that the *minhah* was offered along with the *'olah* and its clear atonement symbolism (Lev. 9:4, 17; 14:10, 20–21, 31; 23:13, 37, etc.). Moreover, the *minhah* accompanied the *'olah* as a regular part of the daily ritual (*tamid*), being offered in the morning and the evening (Num. 28:3–8).

The Meaning of Minhah

Minhah is nowhere used of grain apart from this offering. By itself the word means "gift" or "tribute." The latter use may be clearly seen in the Ehud story in Judges 3:12–30. Because of his people's sin, God had allowed the Moabites under Eglon to oppress the people of God. As their overlord, Eglon was due a certain amount of tribute or "tax money," as the NLT renders it (see vv. 17–18). We see this usage of *minhah* also in the prebiblical Ugaritic texts where, in one of the opening episodes of the Baal epic, the divine council submits to the demands of Yam, the sea god, by offering to deliver up his enemy Baal to him: "Baal is your slave, O Yam, Baal is your slave, O Nahar, the son of Dagon is your prisoner. Even he must bring you tribute, [even he] must bring you gifts [*mnhyk*] like the sons of the Holy One."[1]

This nonreligious context may help us to understand the significance of the *minhah* offering better. It was the gift of vassals to their overlord. We have already noted that sacrifice finds its significance in the light of the covenant where God, the great King, enters into a treaty with his vassal people. The *minhah* was tribute paid to the King, demonstrating the offerers' vassal status. We may thus understand the *minhah* in the book of Leviticus as a tribute offering.

Nevertheless, we must also be aware of a broader use of *minhah* even in the context of sacrifice. Not only does the word in some contexts mean tribute with no reference to ritual, but sometimes the word means sacrifice in general, and in those contexts the word may even refer to a blood sacrifice. Perhaps the most notable example of this use is in the Cain and Abel story in Genesis 4, a passage already discussed. But there even Abel's bloody sacrifice is called a *minhah* (v. 4).

While it is important to be aware of the broader uses of *minhah*, we will focus on the narrow meaning as reflected in Leviticus 2 and as a sacrifice that often was offered along with the *'olah* sacrifice.

The Procedure of the *Minhah* Offering

Two main options presented themselves to Israelite worshipers. They could bring either raw grain (uncooked) or baked bread. The description of the raw grain offering comes first in the text (Lev. 2:1-3). The worshiper was to bring the grain along with olive oil and also incense to the priest. The priest then took a portion—the Hebrew word indicates a small amount like a handful—and mixed it with olive oil and all the incense and burned this mixture on the altar. The incense, as it burned, created an aroma that was "very pleasing to the LORD" (v. 2). The rest of the grain went to the priests, who used it as food. The token of the grain that was burned and the larger part that went to God's servants, the priests, were gifts to God.

The baked bread offering came in many different forms. It could be wafers or a loaf; it could be cooked in a pan or on a griddle. In any case, it was to be made with fine flour and olive oil, but could have no yeast or honey in it (v. 11). The prohibition of yeast and honey is not explained in the text, but there is a consensus about their significance. Students of Leviticus are generally agreed that yeast and fruit honey (the type specified here) were prohibited because they both ferment on burning. The priestly code in Leviticus is consistent in saying that priests should avoid death and decay, and fermentation is a type of decay.

Interestingly, while yeast and honey were forbidden, the ritual insisted on the addition of salt: "Season all your grain offerings with salt, to remind you of God's covenant. Never forget to add salt to your grain offerings" (v. 13). Here we get not only the command but also the motivation. But what was the connection between salt and covenant?

Two other passages in the Old Testament associate covenant and salt. In Numbers 18:19, in the context of establishing Aaron's family as the priestly family, God promises to sustain them by means of the offerings of Israel. It is a covenant promise, and he says that it is a "covenant of salt between the LORD and you and your descendants" (NLT margin). Then in 2 Chronicles 13:5, in reference to the Davidic covenant (2 Sam. 7; 1 Chron. 17), Abijah says, "Don't you realize that the LORD, the God of Israel, made a covenant of salt with David, giving him and his descendants the throne of Israel forever?" (NLT margin).

It is with the word "forever" that I believe we get the significance of the addition of salt to the *minhah*. The *minhah* was a gift from the covenant vassal to the covenant King. The salt represented this covenant and in particular was a memorial to the eternality of the covenant. Salt, after all, does not burn. It doesn't turn into gas; it survives fire intact. Nothing harms salt, just as nothing harms the covenant.

Summary

From its name and the ritual associated with it, we can appreciate the *minhah* as a gift offering. Part was burned and that was the part given to God. Of course, God did not need food to eat. He does not have a body as his human creatures do. The ritual was symbolic and allowed human beings to express their gratitude to God concretely. That is, the *minhah* was an anthropomorphism, a revelation of God himself to us in human form. As the tabernacle/temple was God's home on earth, though we know he didn't actually live in that house, so the *minhah* was a meal for God, though we know he didn't actually eat the grain.[2] Walther Eichrodt explains:

> The whole tenor of ancient Israel's belief in Yahweh is irreconcilable with the idea that God is fed by the sacrifice, bound up as this is with God's dependence on man. The central concept of the

covenant asserts no less than that Yahweh already existed and had proved his power, before ever Israel sacrificed to him. . . . Here the offering of food and drink reminds men that God is the sole giver of life and nurture; and it is for this reason that their gifts to him take the form of the necessities of life.[3]

The largest part of the sacrifice went to the priests. They were God's servants, and so a gift to the priests was, in a sense, a gift to God. They did eat their portion, and they used it to sustain their families. It did serve as food. In Numbers 5:11–31 we have the description of an elaborate ritual by which a man who suspected his wife of adultery could appeal to God in order to learn the truth. In that ritual the husband came with a grain offering and was told not to mix it with olive oil or frankincense (v. 15), presumably because it was not to be burned, but rather to be used for food.

So far we have seen how the *'olah* emphasized the atonement nature of sacrifice, while the *minhah* highlighted that an offering was a gift. As we turn to the third sacrifice in Leviticus, the *shelamim,* we learn of the third characteristic, fellowship.

THE *SHELAMIM* OFFERING

Leviticus 3 (also 7:11–36) presents the instructions for the performance of the *shelamim* offering. Though there are two more offerings yet to describe, the first three form a kind of triad, combining respective emphases on atonement (*'olah*), gift (*minhah*), and now fellowship (*shelamim*). These categories of function were not mutually exclusive, particularly with this third sacrifice, but there is no denying that each had its emphasis. It is therefore not surprising that these three sacrifices were often offered at the same time. Thus, through these three sacrifices, worshipers atoned for sin, offered a present to the Lord, and enjoyed fellowship with God and other worshipers. Again, the text is not interested in explicitly discussing the meaning of the ritual, so we are left to draw some inferences. But the broad outlines of its meaning can be described with certainty.

The Name

There is some discussion over the best translation of the name of this sacrifice. No one questions that *shelamim* is related to the well-known Hebrew noun *shalom*, which means "peace" or "wholeness." Thus, "peace offering" is an appropriate and common translation of this sacrifice. Again, we need to be reminded of the covenantal context and how this word is related to *shalom*. *Shalom*, after all, refers to the condition that results from being in covenant with God. Sin disrupts *shalom*, and so *shelamim* describes the condition that results once that breech has been resolved. As we will see, the sacrifice was a joyous celebration, a kind of religious party, where priests and worshipers enjoyed a sumptuous meal in the presence of God.

The Procedure of the Shelamim Offering

Leviticus 3 has three main sections. In the first part (vv. 1–5), the text describes the sacrifice of a bull or a cow; the second section calls for an animal from the flock; the third specifies a goat, usually considered an animal of the flock.

Interestingly, the preparation for this sacrifice was very similar to the 'olah and may indicate that the *shelamim* also symbolized the atonement of the worshiper. However, as we commented above, the 'olah and the *shelamim* were often offered at the same time. In any case, like the '*olah,* the worshiper presented the animal to the Lord as a gift. It is also interesting that the animal could be either male or female.

The worshiper laid hands on the animal, thus identifying with it before killing it. The blood was then manipulated by the priests; it was thrown on the sides of the altar, which represented the presence of God. At this point, parts of the animal were burned. It is here that the ritual of the *shelamim* departed from that of the '*olah,* since in the latter the entire animal, with the exception of the skin, was burned. In the *shelamim,* only the following parts were burned and given to the Lord: "the fat around the internal organs, the two kidneys with the fat around them near the loins, and the lobe of the liver, which is to be removed with the kidneys" (vv. 3–4, 9–10, 14–15). This prohibition, paralleling the prohibition of eating the blood of the sacrifice, is climaxed by the warning, "Remember, all the fat belongs to the LORD" (v. 16). The fat was the choice part of the animal and was thus given to God. It is theologically significant[4] that the fat of the *shelamim* was placed on top of the '*olah.* Atonement precedes fellowship.

The rest of the animal, whether from the herd or the flock, was to be eaten by the human participants in the ritual, priests (7:28–38) and worshipers (7:11–21). Again, functionally speaking, the *shelamim* was a religious celebration with food, a banquet, so to speak, in the presence of God himself.

According to Leviticus 7:11–21, there were different types of *shelamim,* three in fact: thanksgiving sacrifice, vow, or freewill offering. The first was offered when the individual wanted to thank God for something, perhaps an answer to prayer (Pss. 50:14–15; 107:21–22). The second accompanied the making of a vow to the Lord. And the third implied that the worshiper was moved for no explicit reason to come before the Lord with an offering.

FOR FURTHER REFLECTION

1. How is the *minhah* sacrifice connected to the covenant?
2. Do we offer "tribute" to God in our services today? How?
3. We see that the priest was permitted to use some of the *minhah* as a kind of payment. Is there any connection with the offering taken in churches today?
4. What kind of peace (*shalom*) did the *shelamim* sacrifice celebrate?

9

THE *HATTAT* AND *ASHAM:*
SIN AND GUILT OFFERINGS

⁎⁘⁎

T wo more bloody sacrifices are described in the first part of Leviticus, the *hattat* and the *asham* offerings. There are a number of reasons to treat these two sacrifices separately from the first three. We have seen how the first three form a natural unit with an emphasis on atonement (*'olah*), gift (*minhah*), and fellowship (*shelamim*). Furthermore, the *hattat* and the *asham* are set off from this triad by the noteworthy repetition of "then the LORD said to Moses" at the beginning of chapter 4. The last time that introduction occurred was at the very beginning of Leviticus, just before the first three sacrifices were described. In this way, the narrator separates the first three sacrifices from the next two.

Close examination of all five offerings also reveals that the first three sacrifices were in an important sense voluntary, while the analysis below will show that the *hattat* and *asham* offerings were mandated by certain conditions. For that reason, in the first three sacrifices the focus was on procedure while in the last two it was on the occasions that call for the offerings.

THE *HATTAT* OFFERING

The name of the *hattat* sacrifice is clearly related to the relatively common Hebrew verb *hata'*, which means "miss" or, in its more theologically rich sense, "sin." The doubling of the middle consonant indicates that the noun here might mean to "de-sin" or to "decontaminate," that is, to remove the effects of the sin. In any case, it clearly has to do with the breaking of the law. The specific conditions that are in mind will be discussed below as we spell out the nuances of this text.

Furthermore, we can see that we must understand this sacrifice in the context of the covenant. God had placed certain demands on his people, demands that we usually refer to as law. The breaking of this law created a rift in relationship with God, and sacrifice (as we have described above) was the visible expression of inward repentance or acknowledgment of impurity. The *hattat* sacrifice was a way of restoring relationship with God.

However, there is a question whether we should translate the name as "sin offering" or even "de-sin" offering if sin is understood in a strictly moral sense. After all, some of the conditions that required a *hattat* sacrifice involved not so much morality but ritual uncleanness. *Hattat* offerings were mandated in matters of ritual defilement where the act itself was not morally culpable. An example would have been the sin offering that followed the purification of a man who had a discharge of semen (Lev. 15:13–15) or the offering by a woman at the end of her menstrual period (vv. 28–30). Blood and semen were holy substances associated with life, as well as the sacrificial system and the Abrahamic promise respectively, and therefore were protected by taboos. The menstrual cycle and the emission of semen were not here associated with unethical actions and therefore were not themselves sinful.

Since the *hattat* offering was associated with more than just sinful actions, some have argued that *hattat* might be better understood as a purification offering rather than a sin offering. This offering purified the worshiper and the place of worship of uncleanness.

Inadvertent Sin

Both the *hattat* and the *asham* sacrifices were specifically for *shegagah,* sins committed "in error." The word seems to imply a lack of premeditation, a kind of stumbling into trouble. *Shegagah* is placed in contrast to sins committed *beyad ramah,* often translated "with a high hand" (Num. 15:30 ASV, RSV). The latter clearly refers to blatant, premeditated acts, for which the *hattat* and *asham* sacrifices did not help.

Numbers 35 describes killing that is *shegagah* in verses 22–23:

> But suppose someone pushes another person without premeditated hostility, or throws something that unintentionally hits another person, or accidentally drops a stone on someone, though they were not enemies, and the person dies.

We would call these accidents, things that happen in the course of work, or just life. It was for these that the *hattat* and *asham* applied.

Leviticus 5:1–4 provides further examples. For instance, the *hattat* is for those who touch the body of a dead animal or "come into contact with any source of human defilement" (v. 3). From later Levitical law we can imagine many scenarios that would fit into this category. For instance, a man has a genital discharge and then leaves the room. Another person comes in, sits where he has just sat, and then is informed by another member of the household that the place where he is sitting was defiled (Lev. 15:6). Consequently, the second person is unclean and must go through the proper procedure to become ritually clean again.

Another example in Leviticus 5:4 has to do with someone taking a rash vow, which (presumably) for one reason or another he is unable to keep. The person has good intentions and would follow through if he had the resources, but he doesn't. So he is ritually impure and needs to offer a *hattat* sacrifice.

Even so, such an explanation does not cover all cases of the *hattat* sacrifice. The *hattat* was also for those who witnessed something about which they should have provided testimony in court but didn't. But it is hard to imagine someone doing that totally unconsciously. The conscious nature of some "inadvertent sins" is likewise apparent in examples of offenses for which the *asham* applied. Leviticus 6:1 mentions the case of people who lied that something given into their care had been lost or stolen. Again, it is difficult to understand how this lying could be inadvertent or unconscious.

The great modern Jewish commentator Jacob Milgrom brings his extensive knowledge of rabbinic discussions to this problem. On the basis of rabbinic discussions of Leviticus 5:20–26 and Numbers 5:6–8, he persuasively argues that "repentance of the sinner, through his remorse and confession, reduces his intentional sin to inadvertence, thereby rendering it eligible for sacrificial expiation."[1] Repentance is the key to help us understand the difference between an inadvertent sin and a high-handed sin.

The Procedure of the Hattat Offering

The *hattat* had a basic procedure that varied depending on who was offering it. Earlier, we observed that the *'olah* also allowed for some variety of offerings, but there we suggested an economic reason for the different animals offered. Here, the principle seems to be that the more important the person or group, the more serious the infraction, and therefore the more expensive the necessary offering.

We begin, as the text in Leviticus 4 does, with the high priest, whose offense required the most expensive sacrifice, as well as the most elaborate ritual. The offense of the high priest had the most potential of any individual's offense to cause harm to the community of God. After all, he was the one who offered sacrifices on behalf of the rest of the community. He was the one who penetrated the Holy Place the farthest, even going into the Holy of Holies on the Day of Atonement (Lev. 16).

The high priest was the most important individual in terms of the institutional worship of the Old Testament. As such, the *hattat* offered in response to his sin was the most expensive and intricate, particularly when it came to the manipulation of blood. Earlier, we saw the importance of blood in conjunction with the *'olah* offering, another sacrifice heavily associated with repentance and atonement. Blood represents life, and shed blood represents forfeited life. The sinner deserved to die, but God, in his grace, established a system of animal substitution.

The high priest was required to offer a bull, the most expensive of all sacrificial animals. He came to the entrance of the sanctuary and presented it to the Lord by first of all identifying with it through the laying-on-of-hands ceremony, which again we saw connected to the *'olah* sacrifice. The animal thereby became a substitute for him. Its death stood in place of his death.

The priest on duty then collected and manipulated the blood. Notice that the high priest did not do this himself. Even he needed a human mediator, a role that he had performed himself many times. The priest took the blood and performed three ritual actions with it.

First he put some of the blood on his finger and then, probably through a shaking motion, sprinkled blood seven times on the innermost curtain. This was the farthest that blood was ever taken into the Holy Place, with the exception of the sacrifices of the Day of Atonement (described in part four). That is because the high priest himself penetrated the most deeply into the sanctuary in order to perform his ritual duties. His sin polluted the Holy Place.

Next, the priest dabbed the blood on the horns of the

incense altar. This altar was in the first room of the sanctuary, but at a location near the entrance into the Holy of Holies. This was the only sacrifice where this was done, and its meaning is obscure. M. F. Rooker has suggested that incense represented the prayers of God's people.[2] He is correct to see that this connection is made in a place like Psalm 141:2, but I am not sure that the association is strong enough to make his point with confidence in the context of Leviticus. The remainder of the blood—and the phraseology implies that there was much left—was poured out at the base of the sacrificial altar.

Finally, the fat was removed and burned on the sacrificial altar in a way reminiscent of the *shelamim* offering, regarding which we learned that "the fat belongs to the LORD" (Lev. 3:16). The rest of the sacrifice was carried out to a ceremonially clean location outside of the camp, where it was burned. Apparently, none of the *hattat,* with its emphasis on atonement, was to be used by the priests or the people.

The second category of sinner for which a *hattat* is described was the community as a whole. And on the principle that corporate sin creates a larger harm toward the community than an individual sin, the sacrificial remedy was also severe. As a matter of fact, it was basically identical to that of the high priest. It is possible, but certainly not clear, that this had direct connection to the high priest's sin, which, after all, brought "guilt upon the entire community" (Lev. 4:3).

The third category of *hattat* was offered when a leader other than the high priest sinned. He offered an animal of lesser value than an ox, namely a male goat. In this situation, the blood did not go into the sanctuary proper. Blood was dabbed on the horns of the altar of burnt offering, and the rest was poured at the base of the altar. However, the fat was burned on the altar, just as with the offering of the high priest and the community; and there is surprisingly no mention of what was done with the rest of the animal, though the assumption must be that it too was taken to a ceremonially clean place outside the camp and burned. (Notice, however, Lev. 7:7–10, which implies that it was given to priests.)

The last category includes individuals who were neither priests nor leaders. They could bring a female goat (Lev. 4:28) or female sheep (4:32). The blood and the fat were treated in the same way as in the offering for the leaders, and again there is no mention of what was done with the rest of the animal.

We should note though, that just as with the *'olah*, one could substitute a bird or even grain for an expensive animal like a sheep, ram, or goat according to Leviticus 5:11–13. God is merciful toward the poor as well as toward the rich. Mere possessions do not help or hinder one's relationship with God.

THE *ASHAM* SACRIFICE

The *asham* sacrifice (Lev. 5:14–6:7; 7:1–10) was similar in many ways to the *hattat*. In fact, with one very obvious exception, they were somewhat difficult to distinguish. Indeed, the *asham* and *hattat* also shared similarities with the *'olah*, in that all three had a strong emphasis on atonement for sin. However, the *'olah* was for general sin, while the *hattat* and the *asham* were for specific sins.

These specific sins overlapped. Both categories involved some transgression against the sacred things of the Lord (the technical term is *sancta*). The first line that introduces the *asham* begins, "If any of the people sin by unintentionally defiling the LORD's sacred property . . ." (5:14). Sacred property included most obviously the tabernacle/temple and all the objects associated with it.

Even so, there are difficulties. For one thing, this description does not immediately fit the sins specifically listed in 6:1–7. There we read of such specific sins as lying to a neighbor about an item entrusted to one's care or being dishonest with a security deposit. These examples may not seem related to the "LORD's sacred property," but behind the deception is implicitly the invocation of the Lord's name in an oath. The dishonest neighbor swears by God that something is true when it is not, and so the Lord's name is taken in vain. After all, the Lord's name itself is considered *sancta*.

The Term Asham and Its Procedure

Traditionally, the term *asham* is translated "guilt offering." And this is a good understanding of the term and concept. However, others have argued[3] that *asham* ought to be rendered "reparation offering," which clearly distinguishes the *asham* from the *hattat* and the *'olah* sacrifices.

In a word, the *asham* demanded a reparation, a payment over and above the loss incurred by the transgression. Of course, as an offering that was efficacious for atonement, it involved a bloody sacrifice, in this case of a ram. The ram was slaughtered at the altar outside the tabernacle, and its drained blood was sprinkled against the sides of the altar (7:2). We have already seen that the purpose of such blood manipulation was to highlight the death of the animal in place of the sinner. Again, as with other sacrifices, the fat was burned (7:3–5), but the meat could be eaten by the priests and the males in their family (7:6).

However, above and beyond the slaughter of the lamb, the offerer was to bring a reparation, a payment to compensate for the harm done in the sin. Leviticus 6:5 commands the sinner to "restore the principal amount plus a penalty of 20 percent to the person they have harmed." This payment was unique to the *asham* offering.

The *hattat* and the *asham* offerings complete our look at the five major sacrifices described in Leviticus 1–7. There are other important sacrifices mentioned in other parts of Scripture. For instance, the Passover sacrifice, described in the next chapter, which commemorated the time God killed the first born of the Egyptians but passed by the first born of Israel (see Exod. 12:1–5). Nonetheless, with our exposition of the five sacrifices highlighted in Leviticus, we have the basis on which to go now to the New Testament. There we learn the wonderful truth that Jesus Christ fulfills the entire sacrificial system.

FOR FURTHER REFLECTION

1. What sets the *hattat* and *asham* sacrifices off from the three sacrifices (*'olah, minhah,* and *shelamim*) described in the previous chapter?
2. How are the *hattat* and *asham* related to the covenant?
3. Are there sacred objects (*sancta*) today?
4. Why was it necessary in these cases to add 20 percent reparation? Are there any modern analogies?
5. What is the relationship between repentance and sacrifice? Does this tell us anything about repentance today?

IO

CHRIST: THE ONCE-AND-FOR-ALL SACRIFICE!

✦

The previous chapters have shown that the sacrificial system in Israel during the Old Testament time was wide-ranging and complex. It certainly exerted a significant financial burden on the people. God showed grace, to be sure, in allowing different types of sacrifice, depending on one's economic status, but even a bird cost money! Further, the time burden would have been great, especially for those who did not live in Jerusalem. After all, it was only at the altar in Jerusalem that sacrifices could legitimately be offered. If you lived out of town, the need to sacrifice would have meant traveling to Jerusalem, finding some place to stay, and then traveling back. In addition, for many at least, there would have been a large psychological burden of traveling to the tabernacle/temple in the knowledge of their sin.

The wonderful news of the New Testament is that Jesus has fulfilled the sacrificial ritual by his own death and resurrection. Jesus is the perfect sacrifice, which all the animal sacrifices simply anticipated. In this chapter, we will pursue this important teaching by surveying the variety of passages that make this claim. We will begin with passages that talk in general terms about Jesus as our sacrifice and then continue by looking at Jesus as, specifically, our sin offering, our guilt offering, and our Passover sacrifice.

JESUS, OUR SACRIFICE

The New Testament often connects Jesus' death to Old Testament sacrifice in general terms without using words that specifically identify a type of sacrifice. Even so, it is especially the atonement nature of Old Testament sacrifice that is at issue here. With that in mind, we may especially see the *'olah* as at least implicitly in the background of New Testament writers. However, we did observe in our study of the Old Testament sacrifices that the *'olah, minhah,* and *shelamim* were normally offered at the same time, and so the whole complex may serve as the backdrop of Jesus' sacrifice. Fortunately, our decision on this matter does not radically affect our understanding of Jesus as the fulfillment of the whole sacrificial system.

Jesus' Blood and Sacrifice

> For God sent Jesus to take the punishment for our sins and to satisfy God's anger against us. We are made right with God when we believe that Jesus shed his blood, sacrificing his life for us. God was being entirely fair and just when he did not punish those who sinned in former times. And he is entirely fair and just in this present time when he declares sinners to be right in his sight because they believe in Jesus. (Rom. 3:25–26)

In many other places in the New Testament the blood of Christ is seen as the means by which our relationship with God, shattered by sin, has been restored (see for instance Rom. 5:9). But here Paul specifically connects Jesus' blood to the idea of sacrifice.[1] This association, of course, makes immediate sense against the background of the Old Testament. The blood of the animal, symbolic of its death when shed, represented the death of the sinner who identified with it through the ritual of laying his hands on its head. This connection was purely symbolic, but here in Romans 3:25 we learn that Christ's blood is the ultimate sacrifice that removes from us God's anger for our sins. We are declared righteous because of our union with Christ.

It is important to note that God the Father sent Jesus to perform this act, which removed his anger from us. There is a longstanding debate over whether Jesus' death does away with the wrath of God (propitiation) or simply removes sin (expiation). Romans 3:25 is at the heart of this discussion. Some find the former unflattering of God, and indeed we should note that this passage talks about God sending Jesus. It is wrong to think of Jesus unilaterally pacifying his angry Father by virtue of his death. The three persons of the Godhead work in concert to bring about our redemption. However, we must fully embrace the idea that God (and Jesus, who is of course God) hates our sin, and, though the Father provides the means, Christ's sacrifice does away with that wrath.

Jesus the Spotless Lamb

> For you know that God paid a ransom to save you from the empty life you inherited from your ancestors. And the ransom he paid was not mere gold or silver. He paid for you with the precious lifeblood of Christ, the sinless, spotless Lamb of God. (1 Peter 1:18–19)

In the paragraph preceding these verses, Peter has called for a life characterized by holiness, obedience in spite of the temptations of this life, and hope (vv. 13–17). Starting with verses 18–19, he provides motivation for this life style and attitude by reminding his readers of Christ's great act on the cross, which redeemed them. What draws our interest in these verses is the sacrificial language used here. Our salvation was not paid for by mere money, but rather by Christ's life, which is here described in clearly sacrificial language. He is a lamb without blemish, whose blood, representing his death, earns our redemption. The mention of a spotless animal can be connected to a variety of Old Testament sacrifices, for instance the Passover lamb (Exod. 12:5), the *'olah* sacrifice (Lev. 1:10), a *shelamim* sacrifice (Lev. 3:6), a *hattat* sacrifice, and so on. The effectiveness of the image does not depend on an exact identification with a particular sacrifice. The NLT brings out what is implicit in the characterization of Jesus as without defect; he is, as a human being, without sin. The "sinless" one voluntarily sacrifices himself on our behalf.

Jesus' Sacrifice as Sweet Perfume

> Follow God's example in everything you do, because you are his dear children. Live a life filled with love for others, following the example of Christ, who loved you and gave himself as a sacrifice to take away your sins. And God was pleased, because that sacrifice was like sweet perfume to him. (Eph. 5:1–2)

Paul here states that Christ is a sacrifice who died in order to remove our sins. We have seen this language before and will see it again. What is new is the description of that sacrifice as "sweet perfume" to God. This phrase reminds us that the *'olah* offering provided "an aroma pleasing to the LORD" (Lev. 1:9, 13, 17 NIV).[2] Indeed, the Septuagint translation of the phrase in Leviticus is identical to Paul's words in Ephesians 5:2 (*osmē euōdias*). Paul reminds the Ephesians of the sacrificial nature of Christ's death in order to prod them on to sacrificial behavior themselves. In a later section of this chapter, we will see Paul revisit this language in Philippians 4:18 to describe the behavior of that Christian community.

Jesus' Sacrifice as God's Expression of Love

> My dear children, I am writing this to you so that you will not sin. But if you do sin, there is someone to plead for you before the Father. He is Jesus Christ, the one who pleases God completely. He is the sacrifice for our sins. He takes away not only our sins but the sins of all the world. (1 John 2:1–2)

> God showed how much he loved us by sending his only Son into the world so that we might have eternal life through him. This is real love. It is not that we loved God, but that he loved us and sent his Son as a sacrifice to take away our sins. (1 John 4:9–10)

We can treat these two passages in 1 John together. In both places, Jesus is called a sacrifice (*hilasmos*) for our sins. The use of this term makes these passages appropriate for our survey of New Testament teaching on Christ as our sacrifice. We have already seen a word related to sacrifice (*hilasmos*) above in Romans 3:25. It is, in the words of G. Burge, specifically "a sacrifice to placate someone who is angry." Theologians have debated precisely who or what is placated here. Some say God and others sin itself. I concur with Burge, who is dependent on L. Morris, who makes the commonsensical statement that "sins are covered over and God's righteous anger is changed" by means of this sacrifice.[3] Both of these passages in John describe the basis on which Christians enjoy a restored relationship with God after that relationship has been broken by sin.

Jesus, the High Priest

In chapter 6 we saw how seriously the book of Hebrews takes the priestly theology of the Old Testament and applies it to Jesus Christ. Accordingly, we should not be surprised to observe that the vast majority of passages that describe Jesus as our sacrifice appear in that book. The following passages allow us to capture the flavor of the author's teaching on this subject.

> Now a high priest is a man chosen to represent other human beings in their dealings with God. He presents their gifts to God and offers their sacrifices for sins. And because he is human, he is able to deal gently with the people, though they are ignorant and wayward. For he is subject to the same weaknesses they have. That is why he has to offer sacrifices, both for their sins and for his own sins. And no one can become a high priest simply because he wants such an honor. He has to be called by God for this work, just as Aaron was. (Heb. 5:1–4)

> He [Jesus] is the kind of high priest we need because he is holy and blameless, unstained by sin. He has now been set apart from sinners, and he has been given the highest place of honor in heaven. He does not need to offer sacrifices every day like the other high priests. They did this for their own sins first and then for the sins of the people. But Jesus did this once for all when he sacrificed himself on the cross. Those who were high priests under the law of Moses were limited by human weakness. But after the law was given, God appointed his Son with an oath, and his Son has been made perfect forever. (Heb. 7:26–28)

We will understand these passages more fully after we have studied the priesthood in part three. Right now our attention is riveted on the idea of sacrifice. Hebrews 5 presents the Old Testament situation where even the high priest, the most set-apart of all human beings, needed to offer sacrifices to atone for his own sins. He, after all, was a sinner himself, and since he drew near to God with the sacrifices and gifts of others, his sins needed to be atoned for as well by means of sacrifice. Jesus is a priest of a different order. He is not only the priest but also the perfect sacrifice. He offered this sacrifice of himself for others, not for himself. After all, he is sinless. As the perfect sacrifice, he had to offer himself only once, which our next passage indicates.

Sacrifices and Tabernacle:
Shadows of Jesus and Heavenly Reality

> That is why the earthly tent and everything in it—which were copies of things in heaven—had to be purified by the blood of animals. But the real things in heaven had to be purified with far better sacrifices than the blood of animals.
>
> For Christ has entered into heaven itself to appear now before God as our Advocate. He did not go into the earthly place of worship, for that was merely a copy of the real Temple in heaven. Nor did he enter heaven to offer himself again and again, like the earthly high priest who enters the Most Holy Place year after year to offer the blood of an animal. If that had been necessary, he would have had to die again and again, ever since the world began. But no! He came once for all time, at the end of the age, to remove the power of sin forever by his sacrificial death for us.
>
> And just as it is destined that each person dies only once and after that comes to judgment, so

also Christ died only once as a sacrifice to take away the sins of many people. He will come again but not to deal with our sins again. This time he will bring salvation to all those who are eagerly waiting for him. (Heb. 9:23–28)

The unnamed author of Hebrews recognizes that the Old Testament system of sacrifices was an earthly shadow of heavenly realities. The shadow was a physical tent (the tabernacle) where animals were sacrificed and their blood was manipulated. However, the reality is heavenly, and therefore animal sacrifice simply won't do. It was fine as a symbol, but the reality has to be something much more substantial. And that something more substantial is someone, namely Jesus Christ, who, as we have already seen in Hebrews 7:26–28, offered himself as a sacrifice. And this kind of sacrifice only needs to be offered one time.

The contrast in Hebrews between the inadequate shadows of animal sacrifices and the effective reality of Christ's sacrifice continues in 10:1–18. It wasn't that the animal sacrifices failed in their divinely appointed function; they were instituted after all to be symbols and not the reality. Now that the reality is here, there is absolutely no need for any more animal sacrifices. After all, "when sins are forgiven, there is no need to offer any more sacrifices" (Heb. 10:18).

JESUS, OUR SIN AND GUILT OFFERING

Though most of the relevant passages in the New Testament refer to Jesus as a sacrifice in general terms—at best only hinting at a connection with a particular sacrifice described in Leviticus 1–7—in a few cases there is an apparent identification with the *hattat* or the *asham*. We begin with two passages that speak of Jesus' crucifixion in the language of the *hattat:*

We are Christ's ambassadors, and God is using us to speak to you. We urge you, as though Christ himself were pleading with you, "Be reconciled to God!" For God made Christ, who never sinned, to be the offering for our sin, so that we could be made right with God through Christ. (2 Cor. 5:20–21)

We have an altar from which the priests in the Temple on earth have no right to eat. Under the system of Jewish laws, the high priest brought the blood of animals into the Holy Place as a sacrifice for sin, but the bodies of the animals were burned outside the camp. So also Jesus suffered and died outside the city gates in order to make his people holy by shedding his own blood. So let us go out to him outside the camp and bear the disgrace he bore. For this world is not our home; we are looking forward to our city in heaven which is yet to come. (Heb. 13:10–14)

In the context of the 2 Corinthians passage, Paul urges his audience to be reconciled to God. The basis of this reconciliation is Christ's death. He is the purification offering that removes our sin. He is the sinless sin offering that allows reconciliation with God to take place.

The Hebrews passage is part of the book's concluding emphasis on the benefits of our relationship with Christ. Here, it is specifically the sin offering on the Day of Atonement (see part four) that is meant. The interesting link with Christ's death has to do with the general requirement that the remains of any sin offering be burned outside the city. So the author of Hebrews points out that Jesus was crucified outside the city walls of Jerusalem. He is our sin offering, our Day of Atonement offering. He makes the impure pure again. Not only this, but his death outside the walls of the city also beckons his followers to go outside. Outside the camp is unclean territory, but Christ, having made them holy, tells them to move out.

Most commentators argue that the camp represents the security of Judaism, but now they are to move out into the world for Christ.[4]

JESUS, OUR PASSOVER SACRIFICE

Now the LORD gave the following instructions to Moses and Aaron while they were still in the land of Egypt: "From now on, this month will be the first month of the year for you. Announce to the whole community that on the tenth day of this month each family must choose a lamb or a young goat for a sacrifice. If a family is too small to eat an entire lamb, let them share the lamb with another family in the neighborhood. Whether or not they share in this way depends on the size of each family and how much they can eat. This animal must be a one-year old male, either a sheep or a goat, with no physical defects.

"Take special care of these lambs until the evening of the fourteenth day of this first month. Then each family in the community must slaughter its lamb. They are to take some of the lamb's blood and smear it on the top and sides of the doorframe of the house where the lamb will be eaten. That evening everyone must eat roast lamb with bitter herbs and bread made without yeast. The meat must never be eaten raw or boiled; roast it all, including the head, legs, and internal organs. Do not leave any of it until the next day. Whatever is not eaten that night must be burned before morning." (Exod. 12:1–10)

How terrible that you should boast about your spirituality, and yet you let this sort of thing go on. Don't you realize that if even one person is allowed to go on sinning, soon all will be affected? Remove this wicked person from among you so that you can stay pure. Christ, our Passover Lamb, has been sacrificed for us. So let us celebrate the festival, not by eating the old bread of wickedness and evil, but by eating the new bread of purity and truth. (1 Cor. 5:6–8)

As we deal with the New Testament picture of Christ as our sacrifice, it is absolutely necessary that we introduce another variation on the Old Testament theme of sacrifice, the one connected with the tenth plague against Egypt at the time of Moses. This climactic attack against Egypt and its gods (Exod. 12:12; Num. 33:4) would finally lead to the release of Israel from their slavery in that foreign land. On the night the angel of death came to claim the firstborn of Egypt, Israel was to offer a sacrifice and smear their doorways with the blood and then eat the lamb. While the sacrifice bore some characteristics in common with the Levitical sacrifices described in the preceding chapters, it was unique, and Paul uses this sacrifice in particular to describe Christ's death on the cross.

But Paul is not picking this imagery out of thin air. Indeed, though not stated in so many words, the timing of Christ's crucifixion and indeed the whole structure of his earthly ministry point to the truth that he is the fulfillment of the Exodus; he is the Passover Lamb.

The gospel of Mark (1:2–3) begins with a quotation from Isaiah 40:3 referring to a voice calling in the wilderness. In effect, the opening of the gospel announces that some connection exists between the historical Exodus and Jesus' ministry.

A brief survey of this rich comparison begins with the baptism of Jesus, which parallels the Re(e)d Sea crossing. Paul called the Re(e)d Sea crossing the baptism of the Israelites (1 Cor. 10:1–5). It was the beginning of their redemption, just as Jesus' baptism initiates his ministry.

After the crossing of the sea, the Israelites wandered in the wilderness for forty years. Jesus, remarkably, goes into the wilderness for forty days and forty nights, where he is tempted by Satan (Matt. 4:1–11). More than a superficial numerical coincidence is at work here. Jesus' temptations are the same as those the Israelites experienced in their wanderings. Jesus is tempted in regard to food; the Israelites complained heartily about their lack and quality of food. Jesus resists the temptation to test God; the Israelites were constantly testing God. Jesus rejects Satan's invitation to worship a false god; the Israelites caved in easily to the worship of a golden calf.

Jesus responds to Satan's temptations by quoting the book of Deuteronomy three times, using the speech Moses gave the Israelites just before his death and their entry into the promised land. Moses warned the people not to succumb to temptation as they had in the wilderness. Jesus, by resisting the temptations, shows that he is the obedient Son of God in precisely those areas where the Israelites failed their heavenly Father.

These examples are just the beginning of the Exodus-echoes we find in Jesus. During the wilderness wanderings Moses went up on Mount Sinai and received the law of God. It is more than a coincidence that in the gospel of Matthew (chaps. 5–7) Jesus also goes up a mountain, where he delivers a sermon on the law. Jesus is showing himself to be the divine lawgiver.

There are many more connections, but we are ready to return to our topic. Jesus is crucified during the Passover (John 19:17–37); he becomes our Passover Lamb. What is the Passover but the Jewish festival that celebrates the Exodus? The relationship is undeniable. The Gospels insist that we understand Jesus as the fulfillment of the Exodus and his death as the ultimate Passover sacrifice.

The above survey has no pretensions of being complete. However, the point is well established by this sampling of passages: Jesus is our sacrifice! He is the one anticipated by the symbolic system of Old Testament ritual. With his once-and-for-all sacrifice, there is no longer any need to have any other sacrifice of any kind. As we reflect on the difficulty and unpleasantness of animal sacrifice, we should thank Jesus that he has offered his life as a sacrifice for our sins.

FOR FURTHER REFLECTION

1. Read Isaiah 53, a passage that many Christians say anticipates the coming of Messiah. Notice and reflect on the sacrificial language. How does it relate to Leviticus, and how does it anticipate the New Testament?
2. Read Genesis 22, the story of Abraham taking Isaac to Mount Moriah. Do you note any parallels with Christ's later sacrifice? What do you make of these parallels?
3. Sacrificial language in the New Testament is also used in connection to our response to our new life in Christ. Read Romans 12:1–2; Philippians 2:17; 4:18; Hebrews 13:15; 1 Peter 2:5 and consider implications for our lives.
4. Reflect on the fact that Christ sacrificially died for your sins. What emotional reactions does this evoke from you? How should you respond in terms of your actions?

PART THREE

SACRED PEOPLE

The concept of sacred people is difficult for modern Christians to understand. This difficulty is intensified in the Western world by a strong sense of individualism and democratic ideas that everyone is equal. As we enter the world of the Old Testament, however, it is clear that some people were considered more sacred than other people. Indeed, a whole tribe, the Levites, was set apart or made holy for special service in the Holy Place. Furthermore, within the Levites, one family, the descendants of Aaron, had the superiority.

But does this mean that the Levites and the sons of Aaron were morally or spiritually better than anyone else? Does it mean that they were loved more deeply by God? Here, we encounter another idea that is foreign to a modern audience. Holiness, sacredness, consecration are not primarily moral categories. While priests were expected to be moral people, that was not what made them holy. It was their being set apart for special service to the Lord. The following four chapters explore the concept of priesthood in the Old Testament and show how it anticipated the ultimate Priest, Christ himself.

II

THE RISE OF THE
PRIESTHOOD

✧

At the heart of Old Testament ritual stood the priests. These were men whom God chose to work at the sanctuary and beyond in order to guide his people into his presence. As we have already seen, it was no easy thing to come into the presence of God after the Fall and before Christ. Indeed, it was not only difficult but also dangerous since the unprepared would meet their death. The priests played a very important role, therefore, in the life of ancient Israel.

WHAT MAKES A PRIEST A PRIEST?

Priests may rightly be described as mediators between God and his people. Of course, this description is general and vague, in that not only priests but also kings and prophets may be described as mediating between God and Israel. Priests are commonly distinguished from prophets because they brought the people into the presence of God, while prophets brought God and his word to the people. This distinction holds up as a general principle, but it is certainly not an absolute rule. Indeed, some priests were also prophets, most notably Jeremiah.

In chapter 13 I will offer what I consider a better way of conceptualizing the priestly task—that of the body-guard. But before that, we will explore how the priesthood came into existence in Israel. After all, for much of the Old Testament era, indeed up until the time of Moses, there were no priests in Israel.

THE EARLIEST PRIESTS

The first time the term "priest" was used of an Israelite wasn't until the time of Moses, when it was applied to Aaron and his son. However, before then we see individuals who acted like priests, performing ritual acts such as offering sacrifices at sacred places, particularly altars. These people included Cain, Abel, Noah, Abraham, Isaac, and Jacob.[1]

We may assume that the head of the family, the "patriarch" (used in a broad sense), was the one who functioned as a priest. The oldest man built the altar, offered the sacrifices, and offered his prayers in the presence of God. We may assume that he did this not only for himself but also for his extended family, and in this way he acted like those later identified as priests.

Indeed, we observe an analogy between the transition from patriarch-priests to a separate caste of priests and the transition from altars to sanctuaries. It is, specifically, with the establishment of the tabernacle that we see the ordination of a formal priesthood in Israel, and these two developments came, I suggest, for a similar reason: Israel's size. No longer a large family, Israel was now a nation, and so a priesthood needed to be institutionalized.

Interestingly, as in so many areas, God did not create a whole new institution or system when he brought the priesthood into existence. Indeed, the surrounding nations had priests for centuries before Israel, just as the surrounding nations had kings before Israel. And, basically, the priests performed the same duties as the later Israelite priests. They sacrificed animals, maintained the sanctuaries, and performed divination (see below on the Urim and Thummim). The difference between Israel's priesthood and the priesthood of other nations was not in form, but in content. The Israelite priests served Yahweh the true God, while the priests of Egypt, Mesopotamia, and Canaan served a multitude of false gods.

But this comment leads us to an interesting observation. While no Israelite was called a priest of God before Moses, two non-Israelites were not only called priests, but recognized and affirmed as priests of the true God: Melchizedek, the Canaanite priest-king of Salem (later known as Jerusalem), and Jethro,[2] Moses' father-in-law.

Melchizedek is a shadowy figure in the Old Testament, and since the author of Hebrews develops a complicated analogy between this priest-king of Salem and Jesus Christ, we will reserve our examination of him until a later chapter. Jethro is not developed more fully later, and in some ways he is just as mysterious.

Moses first met Jethro after he fled from Egypt and went into Midian, more specifically the part of Midian in the southeast Sinai wilderness. Jethro is called a priest of Midian in Exodus 3:1, but the text does not specify the deity that he served. To be sure, it is clear that he sacrificed to Yahweh when he heard the good news about God's great acts of deliverance (Exod. 18:7–12), but it is possible, if not likely, that until that point he had been a polytheist and believed in many gods, including Yahweh.

Perhaps the best way to construe the episodic portrait we have of Jethro is to understand that he was a pagan priest when he first met Moses. After he heard of God's great acts, he turned his devotion to Yahweh and offered sacrifices. He did this not as an ordained priest of Yahweh, but rather as patriarch of his clan. Formal priesthood awaited ordination after Moses' trip to the summit of Sinai, and we now turn our attention to that subject.

THE ORDINATION OF AARON AND HIS SONS

Before the Fall, there was no need for a mediator between God and his human creatures. Adam and Eve lived in the presence of God. They both served him in the garden. But after the Fall, as we have seen, it was the responsibility of the patriarch to build the altar and call on the name of the Lord. The very word "altar" in Hebrew (*mizbeah*), furthermore, implies that sacrifices were offered at such locations.

As Israel left Egypt, however, the patriarchal system would no longer suffice. In his wisdom, God called a group of men to serve as his priests. They were to be specially consecrated, set apart for work in the Holy Place of the Lord. Their consecration may be called an ordination, a divine commissioning for a crucial and holy task. In particular, it was Aaron, Moses' brother, and his sons who were chosen for this work.

In one sense, the choice of Aaron is a mystery. No reason is given. He was Moses' brother, to be sure, but that is never cited as a motive for Aaron's ordination. We are first introduced to Aaron at the commissioning of Moses. In Exodus 3 God appears to Moses in the burning bush. When God tells Moses to bear his message of deliverance to his people in Egypt, Moses responds doubtfully. He contends that he is not a speaker who could convince the crowd. Eventually God appoints Aaron to be Moses' spokesman (Exod. 4:16). This episode is never presented as a reason for Aaron's later function as priest, but certainly explains his early prominence in the story of redemption.

There is some question about exactly when Aaron and his sons were ordained as priests. The service that set them apart is recorded in Leviticus 8–9. Earlier in Exodus 29, Moses, on Mount Sinai, received the command to later ordain them and the instructions on how the ceremony should proceed. However, in a tantalizingly brief reference, we hear about priests in Israel even before Moses went up Mount Sinai.

Exodus 19 describes the theophany of God on the mountain and talks about how Israel would encounter their God. Moses went alone at first and heard from God that he would make his presence known to the people more generally. The text records the fear of the people in the face of such a powerful divine appearance, and boundaries between God and the people were clearly established. While Aaron could accompany Moses to the mountain, God proclaimed, "Do not let the priests or the people cross the boundaries to come up here. If they do, I will punish them" (v. 24).

We are left to ask, Who were these priests? How do we fit this reference into the broader narrative? It is a difficult question, and we have to be careful of too facile a harmonization. Indeed, it may be best to leave the question open.

It is possible, however, that the narrative is not given in chronological order. That is, the ordination of Aaron and his sons, but not the whole tribe of Levites (see below), could have taken place before the ascent onto Mount Sinai. Perhaps this would help explain why Aaron was allowed to penetrate so far into the realm of the sacred on Mount Sinai. Furthermore, it may help us to understand better the events of Exodus 32, with the golden calf. If Aaron was already ordained, we recognize why he could easily had led the people in a religious, albeit false, ritual. On the other hand, it is more awkward to think of Aaron being set apart for the priesthood after engaging in such a dubious act. But again, the questions here are not amenable to easy and definitive answers.[3]

In any case, God's command to Moses to ordain

Aaron and his sons as priests is given in the context of the instructions to build the tabernacle (Exod. 29). As will become increasingly clear, the priests were considered part-and-parcel of the tabernacle structure. They would be ritually set apart through the ordination service for work in the tabernacle, which itself had been set apart, and that was the important point to their consecration.

THE ORDINATION SERVICE

The verbs used in Exodus and Leviticus in reference to the initiation of the priests are "purify" (*tahar*), "anoint" (*mashah*), "ordain" (*male'* with *yad*), and "consecrate" (*qadash*).[4] These actions all combined to lift these individuals ritually out of the realm of the everyday, the common, and transport them into the heavenly or sacred. The phrase for "ordain," literally "fill the hand," may refer to payment for the priests, thus showing their full-time devotion to the task, their professional status, so to speak.

The ordination itself was accompanied by four ritual actions: washing with water, putting on new clothes, anointing with oil, and performing certain sacrifices. We will look at these actions in turn, though some are explained much more briefly than the others.

Lustration with Water

The first rite was washing with water, symbolizing cleansing as the potential priest moved from the realm of the common and everyday to the sacred precincts of the temple. Thus, it is appropriate that the washing of Aaron and his sons took place at the entrance of the tent (Exod. 29:4).

Investiture with New Clothing

Next, Aaron was given new clothes to wear. This act of investiture again symbolized the priests' entrance into a new realm. They did not wear the clothes they wore in their old world, but put on new ones that associated them with the tabernacle. Indeed, as Meredith Kline has pointed out, this association is drawn home in that the priestly clothes were similar to the innermost materials of the tabernacle itself.[5]

The clothing itself was "sacred" (NIV) that is, consecrated (*qadash*) according to Exodus 28:2. It was to give the priest "dignity and honor" (also v. 2 NIV). The high priestly garb was quite complex, consisting of "a breastpiece, an ephod, a robe, a woven tunic, a turban and a sash" (28:4 NIV). As with the tabernacle itself, the descriptions of some of these garments are somewhat unclear in matters of detail. However, the overarching purpose of the description is to indicate the priests' connection with the tabernacle.

This connection begins in verse 5 with the general description of the material used to make the clothing: "Have them use gold, and blue, and purple, and scarlet yarn, and fine linen" (NIV). This verse bears comparison with the description of the innermost curtain of the tabernacle as "finely twisted linen and blue, purple and scarlet yarn" (26:1 NIV). One gets the feeling that the priests were mini-tabernacles or, perhaps better stated, that they were part of the tabernacle structure itself. Thus, at their ordination the priests were invested with the symbols that made them one with the sacred space where they would minister.

The ephod seems to have been an outer garment with no sleeves, attached to the body by means of shoulder pieces (28:6–14).[6] It was connected to the breastpiece, which contained the Urim and Thummim, the importance of which to the priestly task will be explained below (28:15–30). Both of these pieces of clothing were made of the ornate material described above. These garments were made of both wool and linen, and their holiness was indicated in that this mixture was forbidden for common use (Lev. 19:19). Both the ephod and the breast-piece carried precious stones said to represent the twelve tribes of Israel. As the priest walked into the Holy Place, he bore the reminder of God's people in their tribal particularity into the divine presence.

The priest also wore a robe of blue (Exod. 28:31–35). We have already seen blue in the other garments, and I should note that blue and purple die were extremely expensive in the ancient world and were thus reserved primarily for royalty. Here the priest reflected the glory of God the King, and so the royal blue was appropriate in this context. Interestingly, the hem of the priestly robe was bordered by golden bells and pomegranates. The latter fit into the garden imagery of the tabernacle and later temple. This was, after all, the garden of God, Eden itself (see chap. 1). The bells are explained by the text: "The sound of the bells will be heard when he enters the Holy Place before the LORD and when he comes out, so that he will not die" (28:35 NIV). This passage accentuates the idea that the tabernacle was a dangerous place, and even the priest needed to tread carefully there. It has also been suggested that in this way the priest is making constant music in the presence of God.[7]

The turban, of course, covered the head, and the high priest's more ornate turban also had a plate of pure gold inscribed with the words "Holy to the LORD" (28:36 NIV). This was a way of continually praising the Lord. The turban and a tunic were to be fine linen, while the sash was the product of an embroiderer.

This lengthy description of clothing in Exodus 28:1–39, refers to the garments of the high priest. Verses 40–41 give a much shorter description of the special, though less-ornate, clothing of the sons of Aaron. The very last clothing described are the linen undergarments that both Aaron and his sons were to wear at all times when they ministered, so as not to incur guilt and die (vv. 42–43).

Anointing with Oil

Anointing was yet a third ritual that lifted the priests out of the realm of the ordinary into sacred space. The anointing was done with oil, and this oil was applied to the priests, their clothing, and the tabernacle. The purpose of this ritual was both to confer God's authority on the priests and to set them off, along with their clothing and the tabernacle complex, as holy. Anointing with oil was not just restricted to priests, but was also used to show God's choice and to confer authority on kings and prophets, as well. Indeed, the verb "anoint" is *mashah* in Hebrew, and "anointed one" is *mashiah*, which forms the basis of the familiar Hebrew word "messiah."

Aaron's anointing with oil showed God's blessing on him and his children. Some passages suggest that the ritual was associated with and perhaps symbolized the recipients' endowment with God's Spirit (1 Sam. 10:6–9; 16:13), which equipped them for their divinely appointed task. Aaron's anointing made such an impression that later, in Psalm 133, it is used as a metaphor for God's abundant blessings:

> *A song for the ascent to Jerusalem.*
> *A psalm of David.*
>
> How wonderful it is, how pleasant,
>   when brothers live together in harmony!
> For harmony is as precious as the fragrant
>   anointing oil
>   that was poured over Aaron's head,
>   that ran down his beard
>   and onto the border of his robe.
> Harmony is as refreshing as the dew from
>   Mount Hermon
>   that falls on the mountains of Zion.
> And the LORD has pronounced his blessing,
>   even life forevermore.

Sacrifices

A number of sacrifices, not surprisingly, also accompanied the ritual of anointing. It began with a sin offering, thus dealing with the potential cultic profanation that Aaron's entrance into the sacred precinct of the tabernacle might have caused. Second, there was a whole burnt offering, an *'olah,* which also was an atonement offering, but had the resonance of a gift as well. Then, finally, the priests were to offer a wave offering (alternatively called an "elevation offering"), which was a type of peace offering (*shelamim,* see Lev. 7:28–38). These were the principal offerings, but there were also daily offerings to be sacrificed on each of the seven days of the ritual. The seven days should remind us of the first week, since creation themes run throughout the descriptions of the tabernacle, which was itself a mini-cosmos (see chap. 3).

While a short statement about the actual ordination of the priests appears in Exodus 40:12–16, the full account of the service is found in Leviticus 8, immediately after the instructions about sacrifices. As with the construction of the tabernacle, described in detail after the instructions, so the ordination of the priests is described in such a way as to emphasize that Moses fulfilled God's wishes to the letter.[8]

Once the ordination took place, the book of Leviticus records that the new priests immersed themselves in their tasks, particularly offering sacrifices (Lev. 9). Despite this good start to the priesthood, trouble was just around the corner. Before looking at the dark side of the priesthood, however, we want to do a fuller examination of their service. As we do, we will see that sacrifices were only one part of their labor for God.

FOR FURTHER REFLECTION

1. Describe the relationship between a patriarchal head of the family and a priest from the post-Moses period.

2. What is ordination? Is the ordination of a minister today the same as the ordination of Aaron? Why is ordination necessary?
3. How do the different steps in the ordination ceremony serve to set off the priests?

12

LEVITES AND THE
PRIESTLY LIFE STYLE

⁘

The Levites were specially set apart for service to the Lord. We will now see how they, along with Aaron, were set apart as the priestly tribe within Israel. But, first, why were they chosen for this special service? The story is one of the more fascinating in the Old Testament and illustrates some important principles of how God works in the world. But it is often overlooked because it is spread out over a number of Old Testament books without explicit reference to each other.

THE RISE OF THE LEVITES TO
PRIESTLY SERVICE

The story begins with the birth of the twelve sons of Jacob. Among the children of Jacob was Levi, from whom the tribe received its name. His birth narrative gives us no clue as to the special status of the later tribe. Levi was the third child of the unloved wife Leah (Gen. 29:34), and he played no special role in the story of Joseph. As one of the brothers who arranged for Joseph's kidnapping to Egypt, he is treated as part of the group, not individually.

However, there is one story in Genesis where Levi played an extremely pivotal role, and that is found in Genesis 34. Jacob and his family were living in the vicinity of the Canaanite city of Shechem. Jacob's daughter Dinah was out in town with some of the young women of the city, and she was seen by the son of the king, who fell in love with her and forced her to have sex. This act was more than a simple urge soon forgotten; he had real feelings for her and asked his father to arrange a marriage for him.

As Hamor, the father, came to Jacob to discuss a marriage arrangement, Dinah's brothers were back from the field and were scandalized to hear that their sister had been forcibly taken by this Canaanite prince. Hamor extended full assimilation privileges to the family of Jacob, and Shechem (not only the name of the town but also of its prince) declared his willingness to do whatever it took or cost for the family to approve this marriage.

It is here that Levi and his brother Simeon saw their opportunity for revenge. They informed Shechem that their custom required circumcision for everyone connected with their family. The circumcision of an eight-day-old baby is one thing, but the circumcision of an adult can be an especially painful matter. Three days after Shechem and all the men of the city underwent this ordeal, Levi and Simeon came and slaughtered them all.

The two brothers achieved their revenge to be sure, but their father Jacob was irate: "You have made me stink among all the people of this land—among all the Canaanites and Perizzites. We are so few that they will come and crush us. We will all be killed!" (Gen. 34:30).

It is hard for modern interpreters to sort out the morality of this story, especially since we hear only the voices of the actors and not the narrator's voice. Perhaps the latter's approval of the brothers' action is seen in that they got the last word in the story. After Jacob's outburst, they responded, "Should he treat our sister like a prostitute?" (v. 31), and the narrative ends.

Whatever the ethics of their action, it continues to have important ramifications, signs of which we encounter next in Genesis 49. This chapter records the last words and testament of Jacob before he died. There we find him blessing some of his children and cursing others. The effects of Jacob's curse on Levi and his cohort in crime, Simeon, reverberate throughout the history of Israel:

> Simeon and Levi are two of a kind—
> > men of violence.
> O my soul, stay away from them.
> > May I never be a party to their wicked plans.
> For in their anger they murdered men,
> > and they crippled oxen just for sport.
> Cursed be their anger, for it is fierce;
> > cursed be their wrath, for it is cruel.
> Therefore I will scatter their descendants
> > throughout the nations of Israel. (Gen. 49:5–7)

The effect of the curse is that in the future Simeon and Levi would have no settled existence. Once the descendants of the twelve sons, the twelve tribes, entered Palestine, they would all get parcels of land—with two notable exceptions. When we fast-forward to Joshua 13–22 and read about the allotment of land to the tribes, our expectations are met, and neither Simeon nor Levi receives any land at all.

Yet, when we think about it, there is a vast difference between the histories of the tribes of Simeon and Levi. The first was given some cities within the tribal allotment of Judah and then slowly over time disappeared as a separate entity. The Simeonites presumably were absorbed into the tribe of Judah. Levi, on the other hand, became one of the most distinctive and important of the tribes. The Levites were given cities throughout the nation, and far from being absorbed, they were one of the most important and colorful tribes in the history of Israel. What was the difference? In a word, the priesthood. How they were set apart for this distinctive service can be seen in Exodus 32, the story of the golden calf.

Exodus 32, a pivotal chapter in the second half of Exodus, focuses on the construction of the tabernacle. Moses was on Mount Sinai receiving the law and the instructions for building the tabernacle, while Aaron, his brother, had given in to the fears and desires of the people. Thinking that Moses had died on the mountain, they took gold, constructed a golden calf, and fell down to worship it. When Moses returned, he was furious and threw the tablets of the law to the ground, breaking them, which symbolized the breaking of the covenant through the act of idolatry.

Suddenly Moses cried out to those who were still loyal to Yahweh, "All of you who are on the LORD's side, come over here and join me" (v. 26). At this, the Levites responded and rallied to Moses' side. He then gave them instructions each to grab a sword and go among their brothers to perform God's judgment. Without hesitation, they began and slaughtered about three thousand idolaters.

For this service, the Levites were set apart to be priests: "Today you have been ordained for the service of the LORD, for you obeyed him even though it meant killing your own sons and brothers. Because of this, he will now give you a great blessing" (v. 29).

The Levites were previously cursed because of their action at Shechem, and in one sense the curse was not overturned. They never received a specific plot of land in the promised territory. However, the curse was transformed into a blessing. They were scattered through the land as a priestly tribe. After all, by their action of killing their brothers and sisters, they showed themselves to be the perfect candidates for the priesthood. For as we will see in the next chapter, the priests were those who protected the Lord's holiness. They were the bodyguards of God.

But before moving on to that subject, let's pause and see how the priests and Levites, having a special status among the people of God, were to live a distinctive style of life.

THE DISTINCTIVE LIFE STYLE OF PRIESTS

The priests had a special status among the people of God. They were chosen and set apart to live in God's presence. Psalm 84 tells us of the joys of living in the sanctuary:

> How lovely is your dwelling place,
>   O LORD Almighty.
> I long, yes, I faint with longing
>   to enter the courts of the LORD.
> With my whole being, body and soul,
>   I will shout joyfully to the living God.
> Even the sparrow finds a home there,
>   and the swallow builds her nest
>   and raises her young—
>   at a place near your altar,
>   O LORD Almighty, my King and my God!
> How happy are those who live in your house,
>   always singing your praises. (Ps. 84:1–4)

With great privilege comes great responsibility. Leviticus 21–22 lists the special requirements demanded of the priests. Of course, they were expected to abide by all the other moral and ceremonial requirements imposed upon the rest of the nation. Those two chapters may easily be divided into six sections, each section concluding with words such as "I, the LORD, am holy, and I make you holy" (21:8; similar wording in 21:15, 23; 22:9, 16, 32).[1]

The first section (21:1–9) is concerned with the topics of mourning and marriage. Priests affirmed life and eschewed death, and so they could not come into contact with dead bodies unless it was a close relative. Furthermore, they could not transform their physical appearance in any way by shaving head or face or by cutting themselves. Since we know that certain Canaanite religious rituals involved self-mutilation, it is tempting to see this whole section (21:5–6) as a polemic against those rituals. It is also true, as we will see below, that the priest had to be "whole" and "without blemish," like the animals they offered on the altar. In marriage, they could not take a prostitute or divorcee.

The second section (21:10–15) addresses the high priest on the same two topics. Because the high priest went even farther into consecrated space, his requirements were even more stringent. He could not even attend to the dead body of his close relatives. He had to refrain not only from cutting off his hair, but even from letting it hang lose. Not only was he to avoid cutting his skin, but he was not even to tear his clothes. And, finally, he could not even marry a widow, let alone a prostitute or a divorcee. His wife had to be a virgin at the time he married her.

In the final section of Leviticus 21 (vv. 16–24), we learn that the priests had to be without permanent or temporary defect. A permanent defect would have been blindness, lameness, deafness, or the like. A temporary defect would have been a broken foot or hand, or scabs, or an oozing sore. God was not unconcerned for these injured or diseased people—he made provisions for them— but they could not officiate at the altar.

The fourth section begins Leviticus 22 (vv. 1–9) and concerns those priests who could not eat priestly food because of their temporary uncleanness. Basically, the text lists forms of impurity described elsewhere in Leviticus, for instance touching the dead (11:39), or having contact with a skin disease (Lev. 13–14) or an emission of semen (15:16).

The fifth section deals with a further issue concerning priestly food (22:10–16): who could eat it besides the priest himself. This food in large part supported not only the priest, but his family, and so this section defines who was considered part of his family. Slaves were included, but not daughters who married outside the priestly circle. Nonetheless, if the married daughter's husband died or divorced her, then she could once again eat this food. The point seems to be that this food was a form of payment to the priests for their service in the sanctuary. The priesthood was, of course, a full-time job, and the priest's household (dependents, including slaves) needed to be supported through the gifts given to the sanctuary.

The sixth section concludes chapter 22 with an emphasis on the need for priests to bring only unblemished animals to the altar (vv. 17–30). God deserves the best, and it would have been tempting on the part of the worshipers to bring defective animals.

All in all, these two chapters in Leviticus indicate that the priests were required to lead a distinctive life style that flowed from their unique responsibility. This realization makes all the sadder the many stories of priests gone bad in the Bible, some of which will be mentioned in the chapters to follow.

FOR FURTHER REFLECTION

1. We have seen how God took something bad and turned it into a blessing for the Levites. As you think about your life, have there been difficult times that God has used for good, particularly for ministry?
2. If God overrules evil for good in our lives, should we feel exonerated for the evil we do?

13

PRIESTLY SERVICE:
GOD'S BODYGUARDS

The Levites' violence against their brothers won them the status of being the priestly tribe of Israel. Their actions were in the service of God; they cleansed Israel of its sin. Moses blessed them at the end of his life, remembering their action and also describing the heart of their future function in Israel's midst:

Moses said this about the tribe of Levi:

O LORD, you have given the sacred lots
    to your faithful servants the Levites.
You put them to the test at Massah
    and contended with them at the waters of
        Meribah.
The Levites obeyed your word
    and guarded your covenant.
They were more loyal to you
    than to their parents, relatives, and children.
Now let them teach your regulations to Jacob;
    let them give your instructions to Israel.
They will present incense before you
    and offer whole burnt offerings on the altar.
Bless the Levites, O LORD,

and accept all their work.
Crush the loins of their enemies;
strike down their foes so they never rise
again. (Deut. 33:8–11)

The poem explicitly acknowledges the Levites' role as guardians. In this case, they are said to have guarded the covenant, which is the legal term that describes Israel's relationship with God. This guardianship then is said to have involved the following elements: (1) teaching the law, (2) sacrifice, and (3) finding out God's will for Israel. Implied in this list is a fourth element, protecting the sanctuary.

TEACHING THE LAW

As the Deuteronomy passage indicates, it was the responsibility of the Levites to teach the people the law. We do not have an exact knowledge of the level of literacy in ancient Israel, and it probably varied throughout the nation's long history, but it was much lower than today. People simply could not be expected to read their Bible every day in order to learn the law. Even if they could read, there would not have been enough copies of the Bible for everyone. After all, the Old Testament period was long before the printing press. We do not have details about the production of copies of the law, but making copies was a slow and laborious process, done by hand and with the utmost care.

For these reasons, the Levites were scattered through the land. The settlement of the Levites is described in Numbers 35:1–8, Joshua 21, and 1 Chronicles 6:54–81. They were given cities among the other tribes and were scattered like leaven throughout the promised land. This way they could be of service to God by providing instruction to all the people.

They, of course, not only taught the law, but they applied it. For example, Leviticus 13 describes the role of the priests as they determined whether a skin disease was such that the diseased person had to leave the camp. They also examined the person's fitness to return to the community, accompanied by the offering of sacrifices.

This important role of the priests and Levites underlines why it was so tragic when they turned against the Lord. When the priests were not teaching people what was right and wrong, then "the people did whatever seemed right in their own eyes" (Judg. 21:25), as the two stories in the so-called appendix to Judges indicate. Both stories start out as family narratives but then escalate into national disasters. The purpose of these stories is to show just how morally, spiritually, and politically dark the period of Judges was.

The first narrative (Judg. 17–18) involves a man named Micah who lived in the hill country of Ephraim. He confessed to his mother that it was he who stole her eleven hundred pieces of silver. She responded to his confession by praising the Lord and using the silver to build an idol! Hardly the right way to praise God, this action reveals just how little teaching must have been going on at the time. One Levite traveling through the area was co-opted to serve as priest at this heterodox family shrine. Even worse, when the Danites showed their lack of confidence in God by moving from their divinely given tribal allotment to an area up north, they induced this opportunity-seeking Levite to go with them in order to serve as their personal tribal priest.

The second story is even more horrifying, if we can imagine that (Judg. 19–21). A Levite living in Ephraim had a concubine who went home to her father in Bethlehem. After a period of time, the Levite traveled down to Bethlehem to reclaim his concubine. On the trip back, they needed a place to stay for the night. Not wanting to stay in Jerusalem, a pagan Canaanite town at the time, the Levite continued on to Gibeah, the future birthplace of Saul. He was shown hospitality by a newcomer to that city, who warned him of the immorality there. Sure enough, that night the men of the city came knocking and insisted on having sex with the visiting Levite. The host refused and instead offered his own daughter and the concubine in order to satisfy the men's sexual lusts. Though in the heart of Israel, Gibeah seems to have been as bad as Sodom and Gomorrah!

The men of the city abused the concubine all night, and she barely had the strength to make it back to the threshold of the house, where she died. The next morning the Levite coldly told her to get up. When she didn't move, he picked her up and took her body back to his home. What he did next is nothing short of grisly. He cut her body into pieces and sent a piece to each tribal leader so as to incite them against the Benjamites. As a result, civil war broke out, but we have seen enough for our purposes.

The period of Judges was a particularly evil period in Israel's history, and the Levites are shown to have been at the bottom of the cesspool. When the teachers of the law are corrupt, we see that the whole nation is effected. The priests were commissioned to teach the law. This way the people would obey God, not infringe on God's holiness.

The unnamed Levites of the book of Judges show us evil priests who not only refused to protect God's holiness but worked against it. The account of Phinehas in Numbers 25 shows us the proper function of the priest. In the immediately preceding chapters, Balak, king of Moab, hired the prophet Balaam to curse Israel as they passed through his territory on the way to the promised land. But because of God's intervention Balaam was unable to curse Israel. Though this strategy failed, another had at least temporary success. Moabite women seduced Israelite men and the latter fell prey to worshiping false gods.

This blatant sin could not go unpunished, and so God brought a plague against the whole community. Thus, when one bold couple "in broad daylight" (Num. 25:4 NIV) entered a tent and began to copulate, Phinehas the priest followed them and skewered them both with one thrust of his spear. The plague stopped, and God entered into a covenant with Phinehas "because he was zealous for his God and made atonement for the people of Israel" (v. 13).

SACRIFICE

In part two, we took a close look at sacrifices in the Old Testament. Sacrificial offerings were necessitated by the sin of God's people. Sin broke the covenant, rendered the people unclean, and accordingly was an assault on God's holiness. In addition, the book of Leviticus erected a complex symbolic system of ritual cleanness. Many of these laws of purity did not keep Israel from sin so much as they protected important substances that represented life, such as blood or semen; or else they taught Israel other important truths, such as the need for God's people, the Israelites, to keep their distance from other people, the Gentiles.

The regulations concerning unclean food are examples of such laws. Sin and uncleanness threatened God's holiness, and sacrifice was God's means of restoring *shalom* in the camp. As we have seen, the priests in particular were responsible for administering the sacrifices. In this way, they protected God's holiness.

DISCERNING THE WILL OF GOD

As we observed in the blessing in Deuteronomy 33, the high priest was entrusted with the means of asking

God questions that would determine the actions of the people of God. The Urim and Thummim were a two-part device whereby the people of Israel could solicit guidance from God. In an important way, we should view this function of the priesthood as an extension of their teaching of the law. The law was an expression of God's will for his people's behavior. However, the law did not cover every occasion, and often when a question arose as to God's will in a particular circumstance, the high priest would have recourse to the Urim and Thummim.

An example may help clarify. First Samuel 23 narrates the time when David fled from a jealous Saul. David was wandering the countryside, but he was not powerless. In fact, he was more like a nation in exile. He had a standing army, a prophet, and a priest in attendance. Abiathar, the priest, had come and brought with him the ephod, a garment that contained the Urim and Thummim.

On the day reported in 1 Samuel 23 David heard that the Philistines were stealing grain from the people who lived in the Judaean town of Keilah. He wanted to intervene and save them, but as a devout leader he wanted first to know God's will in the matter. The text tells us that he asked God, who responded positively. However, David's men were not so sure, and so David inquired of the Lord a second time. As expected, God told him to go to Keilah. At the end of this interchange, the narrator provides the reader with an explanatory note: "Abiathar the priest went to Keilah with David, taking the ephod with him to get answers for David from the LORD" (v. 6). This note tells us how David received answers. As the story continues, David had occasion to ask the Lord more questions, and through Abiathar's use of the ephod that carried the Urim and Thummim, he got answers from God.

But now let's look more closely at the Urim and Thummim. What was it and how did it work? We get a description of sorts in Exodus 28:30. We are not told what the Urim and Thummim looked like. What we are told is that they were placed in a pocket on the chest-piece, presumably attached to the linen ephod, which the high priest wore while serving at the sanctuary. Exodus 28:30 explains the reason the ephod was carried there. "[It is] to be carried over Aaron's heart when he goes into the LORD's presence. Thus, Aaron will always carry the objects used to determine the LORD's will for his people whenever he goes in before the LORD."

The name Urim and Thummim is Hebrew for "Lights and Perfections." We do not know what this device looked like or how it worked. A survey of its use shows that it answered specific questions with yes, no, or silence. Occasionally, additional revelation accompanied the yes or no. Numbers 27:21 gives us a picture of how the device was to be used: "When direction from the LORD is needed, Joshua will stand before Eleazar the priest, who will determine the LORD's will by means of sacred lots. This is how Joshua and the rest of the community of Israel will discover what they should do."

The relationship described here between Eleazar and Joshua characterized the intended relationship between the high priest and the political leader throughout the history of Israel. In this way, the priests functioned as protectors of God's holiness, keeping Israel from falling into sin that would alienate them from their God.

Later in his life, Joshua provided an illustration of the dangers of not discovering God's will. Israel's entry into Palestine after forty years in the wilderness began with great success. God the warrior gave them victory over the most powerful city in the region when they defeated Jericho. However, they initially lost to Ai, a town whose very name means "dump." After discovering the sin that led to their defeat and executing the culprit, they defeated that city.

Then they were approached by a band of sojourners who looked as if they had traveled long and hard to reach them. Their clothes were tattered and their food was crusty. They told Joshua that they had come from outside the land in order to submit themselves to Israel. Since Deuteronomy 20 allows for alliances with people from outside the land, Joshua agreed to the relationship. If the travelers had been from within Palestine, Israel would have been under very strict divine orders to eradicate them. After all, Israel was not just winning a land for themselves; they were also God's tool of judgment against a particularly sinful people.

But Joshua had been deceived! The weary-looking travelers were from right around the corner. They should have been executed, but now it was too late. The Israelites had given their word. The narrator locates the heart of the problem in the fact that Joshua did not ask God, as Numbers 27:21 dictates and David in 1 Samuel 23 illustrates. Instead, "the Israelite leaders examined their bread, but they did not consult the LORD" (Josh. 9:14). They should have asked God, and if they had, they would have done so through the priests, the protectors of God's holiness.

GUARDIANS OF THE SANCTUARY

Perhaps the most obvious way that the priests and Levites protected the holiness of God is that they were the ones through whom other Israelites had to pass in order to gain access to the Holy Place. We see this through the arrangement of the camp as described in Numbers 2. This chapter strikes most modern readers as tedious and is frequently passed over. On the contrary, the arrangement of the camp is a statement of profound theological significance.

In the first place, note that the tabernacle was in the center of the camp with the tribes in their assigned locations around the tabernacle. Above, we observed that this central location was because God is the King, the divine warrior. And like an ancient Near Eastern king camped with his army, God was in the center. More pointedly for our discussion, it was specifically the Levites who immediately surrounded the tabernacle, the place where the king's personal troops, his body-guard would have been. Any attack on the camp that tried to reach the king would encounter the most severe resistance.

THE NAZIRITES: LAYPRIESTS

The priests and Levites were "set apart" or conse-crated for special service to the Lord. This consecration was a permanent state for the individuals involved, and their special status was passed down genealogically from father to son. In the Old Testament, a clear and definite distinction existed between the priests and the rest of the people of God. To be sure, in comparison to other nations Israel itself could be called a "kingdom of priests" (Exod. 19:6), but among the Israelites themselves the Levites held a distinctive and obvious place.

Nevertheless, tucked away in the book of Numbers is a law that allowed laypeople, men and women, to dedi-cate themselves in a priest-like way. Numbers 6:1–21 de-scribes the Nazirite vow, which resulted in Israelites "setting themselves apart to the LORD in a special way" (v. 2). The term "Nazirite" itself comes from a verb that means "dedicate oneself to a god." An individual could take this vow, or else a mother could dedicate a child in this way, but it came with special requirements for the Nazirite no matter who took the vow. These special re-quirements were similar to the requirements imposed upon priests.

In the first place, the Nazirite could not consume in-toxicating drinks (vv. 3–4). This regulation resembled the one that instructed priests not to drink while they were ministering at the sanctuary (Lev. 10:9). The Nazirite vow, however, was much more severe than that covering the priests. First of all, during the period of their Nazirite vow, individuals were never allowed to drink wine, while for the priests it was only during the time they were working. Second, in what almost seems like a legalistic fencing of the law, the Nazirite could not have anything to do with the grape that produced wine. They could not drink grape juice or eat grapes or raisins. In other words, this vow was not to be taken lightly; it involved real sacrifice in terms of life style.

In the second place, Nazirites could never cut their hair (Num. 6:5). Indeed, if we translate the Hebrew phrase *pera' se'ar* in its full sense of "loose, unkempt hair" (rather than simply "hair," as in the NLT), it appears that the devotees were not permitted even to touch their hair, again a kind of heightening of the law. This regulation connects to the idea that priests should not associate with the realm of the dead. There was a sense in which cutting the hair left one holding dead matter, and this was symbolically prohibited of those who were consecrated to God. The long hair of the Nazirite thus became symbolic of his or her vow and thus any defilement of the vow was spoken of as defiling the hair.

The prohibition from having contact with the dead becomes explicit in Numbers 6:6–12. Even if a family member dropped dead, Nazirites were not to go near the body. On the off chance that someone died suddenly in their presence, they were to shave off their hair, offer sacrifices, and renew their vows.

From the description in Numbers 6, it appears that most people who took the Nazirite vow did so for a brief period of time. This time period could apparently be of any length, but later Jewish tradition states that a typical duration was about thirty days (Mishnah, *Nazir* 1:3).[1] The motivation for taking this vow was likely one of devotion to God, wanting to be close to God in a special way. Once the vow was completed, then the Nazirite went to the priests and offered a series of sacrifices. Interestingly, these sacrifices were similar to those performed for the dedication of Aaron and his sons (burnt offering, sin offering, and peace offering).

Even though Numbers 6 describes a temporary vow, examples from the historical books record the appearance of life-long Nazirites. Two are well known—Samuel (1 Sam. 1:11) and Samson (Judg. 13:4–14)—and in both cases their mothers dedicated them before birth with vows if God would allow their barren wombs to give birth.

Particularly in the latter story the Nazirite vow played a major role. Knowing the requirements for a Nazirite according to Numbers 6 helps the reader realize just how callous and indifferent Samson was to the vow and therefore to his God. He was not to touch a dead body, but he scooped honey out of a lion carcass and used the jawbone of a donkey as a weapon. Furthermore, in response to Delilah's nagging, he said that she should tie him with seven bowstrings, which would have been made of animal gut (Judg. 16:8). And of course, everyone knows the scene of Samson's capture, where out of pride he told Delilah that he would be weakened by having his hair cut. God overruled Samson's evil and indifference, using it to bring about a significant victory over Israel's oppressors, the Philistines.

Thus, a knowledge of the Nazirite vow enriches our understanding of the theme of the Samson story.

FOR FURTHER REFLECTION

1. How does God's holiness manifest itself in our world today? Who guards God's holiness today?
2. What does it mean for a person to be holy?

3. Are ministers more holy than laypeople in today's church? Is anyone more holy than anyone else?
4. It was the priest's role to teach the people the law. Where do we learn of God's will today?

14

JESUS, THE
ULTIMATE PRIEST

✦✦✦

Up to this point in our study of Old Testament worship, we have seen that both sanctuary and sacrifice lead us ultimately to Jesus Christ.[1] He is the very presence of God, and it is his sacrifice on the cross that the animal sacrifices merely foreshadow. First Peter 1:10–12 captures well the idea that Christ is the ultimate fulfillment of the Old Testament message as a whole:

> This salvation was something the prophets wanted to know more about. They prophesied about this gracious salvation prepared for you, even though they had many questions as to what it all could mean. They wondered what the Spirit of Christ within them was talking about when he told them in advance about Christ's suffering and his great glory afterward. They wondered when and to whom all this would happen.
>
> They were told that these things would not happen during their lifetime, but many years later, during yours. And now this Good News has been announced by those who preached to you in the power of the Holy Spirit sent from heaven. It

is all so wonderful that even the angels are eagerly watching these things happen.

But it is the book of Hebrews that relates the wonderful message that Jesus is the ultimate High Priest, just as it connects him to many other matters in Old Testament worship. Though we might expect Hebrews to proclaim the connection between Jesus and the Old Testament priesthood, we are not prepared for the particular shape of his argument. According to Hebrews 4:14–8:14, Jesus is a High Priest like no other. He is a priest according to the order of Melchizedek.

WHO WAS MELCHIZEDEK?

Melchizedek was a shadowy figure when introduced in Genesis. Genesis 14 narrates the raid of four Near Eastern kings into Canaan, where the patriarch Abraham had taken up residence. It is unlikely that this was a major invasion; it seems more like an attempt to achieve some quick plunder and leave the area. The invaders fought and defeated five Canaanite kings and carried off the spoils of their conquest. Unfortunately for them, these spoils included a prisoner of war named Lot, Abraham's nephew.

When Abraham heard of Lot's capture, he rallied his men, 318 of them, and set off in hot pursuit. He caught up with the Near Eastern kings, routed them, and recovered all the plunder, including Lot.

It is on his return to Canaan that Abraham encountered Melchizedek. First came the king of Sodom, perhaps the leader of the five-king coalition of Canaan. He was understandably grateful to Abraham for his recovery of the plunder. At the same time, Melchizedek appeared, seemingly and notably out of nowhere. He is described as the "king of Salem," which was likely the later

Jerusalem. His name means "King of Righteousness," and his title could be translated "King of Peace."

It is difficult to know what to make of this. The interchange between Melchizedek and Abraham is tantalizingly brief. We are left with many questions.

In the first place, Melchizedek is not only called "king of Salem," but also "priest of God Most High" (*'el 'elyon*: Gen. 14:18). Tellingly, Abraham recognized Melchizedek as a fellow worshiper. He treated him as an authority figure, someone who deserved his great respect. This is important to recognize because we are surprised to find a Canaanite king who worshiped the same God as Abraham, and Abraham's actions give him credence in our eyes. Up to this point in the patriarchal narrative, we have heard of no one outside of Abraham's family who shared their faith in the true God.

Scholars have further pointed out that the divine name associated with Melchizedek is not one that was narrowly associated with Abraham's God. Indeed, *'el 'elyon* was a common epithet for the head of the Canaanite pantheon, who is known from ancient texts as *El*. Some people use this to suggest that the distinctive faith of the Old Testament developed out of a common background in Canaanite religion. However, such a viewpoint does not sit well with the biblical narrator's silent approval of Abraham as he submitted himself to Melchizedek's authority by receiving his blessing and then giving him a tenth of the plunder.

As a matter of fact, Abraham's approval and alliance with Melchizedek is contrasted with the way he treated the king of Sodom. The latter was grateful for Abraham's recovery of the people who had been captured by the Near Eastern kings. He enthusiastically expressed his appreciation by allowing Abraham to keep the plunder for himself, returning only the king's captured subjects. But Abraham wanted nothing to do with the king of Sodom and would keep absolutely nothing associated with him (Gen. 14:22–24).

This short episode is the only place where we get a historical insight into the figure of Melchizedek. When we are done reading it, we are honestly left scratching our heads. Who was this man who appeared virtually out of nowhere and received such great respect and honor from no less than Abraham?

PSALM 110

Before returning to Hebrews, we need to take a short stop in the book of Psalms. Melchizedek, after all, is mentioned in one other place in the Old Testament, Psalm 110. But those who are looking for answers to some of the questions raised in Genesis 14 will be disappointed. Indeed, Psalm 110 will raise even more questions and difficulties!

In the first place, there is a debate over who is being addressed in the psalm. It begins,

> The LORD said to my Lord,
>   "Sit in honor at my right hand
> until I humble your enemies,
>   making them a footstool under your feet."
>   (Ps. 110:1)

Most scholars believe, as I do, that God is addressing the Israelite king David and his descendants here. The psalm in its ancient setting was likely a coronation song. Others, however, believe that the psalm is a messianic psalm in the sense that is narrowly prophetic. In such a case, it would have no ancient reference but would have its only fulfillment in Christ.

This latter view is both unlikely and unnecessary. It is unlikely because it would be the only psalm that would have no Old Testament background. Since it is a difficult psalm to translate and understand, it would not be a good idea to make this psalm an exception to the rule. Nor is it necessary. It is better to think that as Hebrews associates Christ's name and function with Melchizedek, this connection flows from Psalm 110:4, where God says, "You are a priest forever in the line of Melchizedek." After all, Christ is a descendant of David, in fulfillment of prophecy, and indeed, David's "greater son" (Matt. 21:41–46). Therefore, this royal coronation hymn is naturally applied to Christ as a descendant of David—indeed his most important descendant—though, as previously stated, its Old Testament application was originally to David and his dynasty.

JESUS, HIGH PRIEST ACCORDING TO THE ORDER OF MELCHIZEDEK

Before continuing with a more in-depth look at the teaching of Hebrews, let me say that it is precisely the mystery of the two Old Testament references to Melchizedek that appeals so much to the author of Hebrews. The author exploits the ambiguities about the Old Testament figure in order to make his important point concerning Christ as priest. He is an exalted priest—so exalted that he transcends the normal categories. He is so much better than Aaron, the priests, and the Levites that he is of a whole different order.

It is not the purpose of the author of Hebrews to tell us more about the Old Testament figure Melchizedek, and he is clearly not saying that Melchizedek was a pre-incarnate appearance of Jesus. The author's allusion to Melchizedek is his way, in keeping with first-century literary practices, of saying that Jesus is the priest par excellence.

With this in mind, we will follow the argument of Hebrews in regard to Jesus as the ultimate High Priest.[2] Hebrews 4 begins by describing the future rest that God provides for those who follow him. But the tone is one of warning about the possibility of God's judgment. The author's audience is told to "tremble with fear that some of you might fail to get there" (Heb. 4:1). This section concludes by describing how God's Word exposes our souls with surgical precision. "It exposes us for what we really are" (v. 12). Our God is a God of judgment and justice.

Once this somber note of warning is given, Hebrews turns to the comforting thought that Jesus is there for us. Hebrews 4:14 says, "That is why we have a great High Priest who has gone to heaven, Jesus the Son of God." The road is hard but Jesus is there to bring us spotless before God.

A priest is someone who brings the people before God. He also brings the people's gifts to God. Aaron and his sons did that, and now Jesus does that as well. Hebrews further informs us that Jesus, just like human priests, experienced temptations. Since we all are tempted, the priests are one with us and can well represent who we are.

However, it is precisely at this point that Hebrews points to the huge difference between Jesus and typical human priests. The priests were tempted and often fell into sin. Jesus was tempted, but never sinned. He is a sinless priest. This has monumental ramifications. Priests not only offered sacrifices for the people; they had to offer sacrifices for themselves as well. In part four, we will see that this was true even for the high priest on the Day of Atonement. Jesus, though, does not have to offer sacrifices for his own sins. He has none. He exclusively represents *us* before God.

It is at this point that the author associates Jesus with the priestly order of Melchizedek for the first time. After quoting Psalm 2 and thus identifying Jesus as God's Son, he cites Psalm 110:4, which we have seen above: "You are a priest forever in the line of Melchizedek" (Heb. 5:6).

Before developing the relationship between Jesus and Melchizedek, the author urges the reader to move from the simple things of the faith (milk) to the more complex concepts of a mature believer (solid food). While not making an explicit connection, the context suggests that the relationship between Christ and the enigmatic figure of Melchizedek is no simple teaching. Those who have easy answers to the questions of this passage (for instance, insisting that Melchizedek is really Jesus) go against the tone of this admonition.

We return to the subject of Melchizedek at the end of Hebrews 6, and it is developed in chapters 7 and 8. It begins with an interpretive recap of Genesis 14 and the encounter between Abraham and Melchizedek. However, there is an interpretive slant that we will now bring to the fore.

Hebrews 7:3 comments that the priest-king of Salem was "without father or mother, without genealogy, without beginning of days or end of life, like the Son of God he remains a priest forever" (NIV). If we read this statement with modern lenses on, we will misunderstand it to say that Melchizedek was not born in a human way and is still alive. But if we put ourselves back into the ancient world that produced Hebrews, we will know that the author is speaking about Melchizedek as a literary figure. Nowhere is his birth or death recorded. He pops into the narrative in Genesis and pops right out again. The author of Hebrews exploits this literary fact in order to make the overriding point that Jesus is better than Levi and his priesthood surpasses the Levitic priesthood.

Indeed, the text is saying that Melchizedek was Abraham's superior! Abraham was the father of the faith, but he submitted himself to Melchizedek. Again, according to first-century Jewish thinking, if Abraham bowed to Melchizedek in homage, so Levi his descendant, a product of his loins, so to speak, also showed his obeisance to Melchizedek. This is the force of Hebrews 7:9–10:

> In addition, we might even say that Levi's descendants, the ones who collect the tithe, paid a tithe to Melchizedek through their ancestor Abraham. For although Levi wasn't born yet, the seed from which he came was in Abraham's loins when Melchizedek collected the tithe from him.

The association between Christ and Melchizedek rather than Levi also helps the author of Hebrews explain one other well-known fact. An Aaronic priest was a descendant of Levi, while Jesus was from the royal tribe of Judah. Associated with this is the fact that Melchizedek was not only priest, but also king of Salem. There was a clear and important distinction between priests and kings in Israel. Indeed, Saul got himself into a lot of trouble by offering sacrifices (1 Sam. 13).

The teaching of Hebrews is summarized by the statement that begins chapter 8: "Here is the main point: Our High Priest sat down in the place of highest honor in heaven, at God's right hand. There he ministers in the sacred tent, the true place of worship that was built by the Lord and not by human hands" (vv. 1–2). This passage combines the teaching about place of worship with the agent of worship. Indeed, it continues by talking about the mode of worship—Jesus goes to the sacred tent to offer sacrifice.

The remarkable teaching of the Bible is that Jesus provides all the resources we need for the worship of God. He is the place of worship, as well as the means and the mode of worship. Hebrews in particular tells us that Old Testament worship has been superseded, and priests like Aaron and his sons are no longer required. When we study the Old Testament, we see that there was indeed a large gap between the people and those who ministered at the sanctuary. The New Testament tells us that we are a "priesthood of priests" (1 Peter 2:4–12, esp. 9), and thus no one is holier than anyone else. As the Pastoral Epistles tell us, there is still a hierarchy of sorts in the church, but not along the same lines as the Old Testament. Christ is our one and only priest, who leads us into the very presence of God.

FOR FURTHER REFLECTION

1. Reflect on how Christ functions as a priest in your life.
2. How does Christ protect God's holiness?

PART FOUR

SACRED TIME

We come at last to the fourth dimension of Old Testament priestly theology. Sacred time is time set apart for rest from daily work and for special worship of the Lord. At the sanctuary, every day was sacred time, as was indicated by the daily sacrifices. The priests were instructed (Exod. 29:38–46; Num. 28:1–8) to present a set sacrifice in the morning and in the evening. At each of these sacrifices, one lamb was to be offered, along with a mixture of two quarts of grain and one quart of olive oil. To complete this twice-daily sacrifice, they were also to pour out one quart of wine before the Lord. These sacrifices were also called the *tamid* or "continual," since they were continually, that is daily, offered to God.

In the chapters that follow, we will concentrate on the special holy days of the Old Testament to understand their purpose better. We learn about most of them from the first five books of the Old Testament (called the "Pentateuch"), in particular the so-called festival calendars (Exod. 23:14–19; Lev. 23; Deut. 16), as well as a list of festival sacrifices (Num. 28–29). The main Pentateuchal sacrifices were the three pilgrimage festivals (*haggim*): Passover with Unleavened Bread, Harvest or Firstfruits, and Tabernacles. Further, we will look at the very important ritual of the Day of Atonement, as well as the briefly described

Festival of Trumpets that preceded it. In a sense, all of these festivals were extensions of the Sabbath, and so we begin with a look at the Old Testament Sabbath. We will extend our study with a short examination of the one and only post-Pentateuchal festival, Purim.

15

THE SABBATH:
THE FOCUS OF SACRED TIME

The Sabbath is, if not the most important, certainly the most foundational of sacred times in the Old Testament. It is frequently mentioned in the Scriptures, and so an exhaustive discussion of the institution is not possible in a book this size.[1]

Sabbath observance is also a hotly debated issue among many Christians even in the twenty-first century. A number of devoted believers suggest that the Sabbath is still to be observed today, and to "break" the Sabbath by working or by nonreligious recreation is a serious offense against God, as well as a cause for many of today's social and psychological problems.

A large number of other faithful and Scripture-loving people believe that the Sabbath is a thing of the past, and to observe the Sabbath is an act of legalism, that is, creating human laws and asserting them with the force of divine law.

Some Christians believe that the Sabbath is the only time that is still sacred or set apart for special observance. It is a virtually universal belief that the other festivals and celebrations are relegated to the past as fulfilled in Christ. With the possible exception of the Sabbath, to be discussed below, all time is considered as holy as any other. This is because we now live constantly in the presence of Christ.

We begin with a survey of what the Old Testament teaches us about the Sabbath. What is it, how was it established, and how was it observed?

PENTATEUCHAL FESTIVAL CALENDARS

We start our exploration with the calendars that enumerate the festivals found in the Pentateuch (also called the Torah). We start here for no better reason than that we will use these calendars to structure our discussion of all the festivals in this section, at least those mentioned in these first five books of the Old Testament. In particular, we will use Leviticus 23, the most extensive of the lists of sacred times, as our focal point from which we will branch out and examine the concept and institution of Sabbath in the Old Testament. Here the Sabbath stands at the head of all the other festivals.[2] It is the first mentioned, and the argument could be made that the other sacred times flowed from the Sabbath. Some of the other festivals actually incorporated Sabbaths within their celebrations.

In Leviticus 23:1-3, the introduction to the calendar is immediately followed by a description of the Sabbath:

> The LORD said to Moses, "Speak to the Israelites and say to them: 'These are my appointed feasts, the appointed feasts of the LORD, which you are to proclaim as sacred assemblies.
>
> " 'There are six days when you may work, but the seventh day is a Sabbath of rest, a day of sacred assembly. You are not to do any work; wherever you live, it is a Sabbath to the LORD.' " (NIV)

The seventh day of every week is a Sabbath. The English word is formed from the Hebrew *shabbat* or *shabbaton,* derived from the verb *shabat,* which means "cease, rest." The word thus highlights one of the main characteristics of the day—the cessation from regular work.[3] Indeed, throughout the Old Testament the emphasis is on rest from work, with only occasional mention of special acts of worship performed on this day.

But why is this day considered so special? Why is the seventh day a day of rest? The Bible actually gives us multiple answers to this question, grounding the practice of Sabbath rest in law, creation, redemption, and covenant.

THE LAW OF THE SABBATH

The importance of the Sabbath becomes clear when we read the legal portions of the Pentateuch. In the first place, it is the only ritual action that finds a place in the Ten Commandments. Soon, we will discover that the fourth commandment, the one concerning the Sabbath, has distinct forms in the books of Exodus and Deuteronomy. But there is enough similarity for us to cite only the first here and reserve the second for later:

> Remember to observe the Sabbath day by keeping it holy. Six days a week are set apart for your daily duties and regular work, but the seventh day is a day of rest dedicated to the LORD your God. On that day no one in your household may do any kind of work. This includes you, your sons and daughters, your male and female servants, your livestock, and any foreigners living among you. For in six days the LORD made the heavens, the earth, the sea, and everything in them; then he rested on the seventh day. That is why the LORD blessed the Sabbath day and set it apart as holy. (Exod. 20:8–11)

The Ten Commandments are the fountainhead of biblical law. They are the ground principles from which all the other laws flow (i.e., Exod. 20:22–23:19). The latter laws, as well as the similar laws in Leviticus, Numbers, and Deuteronomy, may be traced back to and seen as particular expressions of general laws found in the Ten Commandments.[4] The inclusion of the Sabbath law in the Ten Commandments underlines its importance and encourages us to reflect on the Sabbath's continuing relevance for today.

The laws and stories that follow the giving of the Ten Commandments help us understand how the Sabbath was observed and regulated during the Old Testament era. Again, this structure emphasizes the Sabbath's importance as well as its connection with the covenant.

SABBATH AND COVENANT

The law of the Old Testament is not a prerequisite for membership among God's people. The Old Testament never teaches that one has to obey God to earn a relationship with him. God saves his people by grace, and then he gives them laws, which they are supposed to obey to live out that relationship.

The most pervasive metaphor describing the relationship between God and his people is the covenant. "Covenant" is a legal term, reflecting the Hebrew term *berit,* but more specifically the Hebrew term should be understood as indicating a treaty, a treaty between a great King, God, and his servant people, Israel. In ancient Near Eastern treaties, the great king would impose legal requirements on his servants, along with punishments for disobedience. Indeed, studies have shown that many covenant texts of the Old Testament have a vague literary resemblance to ancient Near Eastern treaties that have been recovered from antiquity and translated into English.[5]

Observance of the Sabbath is one such covenant requirement. In fact, it is singled out in Exodus 31:13–17:

Tell the people of Israel to keep my Sabbath day, for the Sabbath is a sign of the covenant between me and you forever. It helps you to remember that I am the LORD, who makes you holy. Yes, keep the Sabbath day, for it is holy. Anyone who desecrates it must die; anyone who works on that day will be cut off from the community. Work six days only, but the seventh day must be a day of total rest. I repeat: Because the LORD considers it a holy day, anyone who works on the Sabbath must be put to death. The people of Israel must keep the Sabbath day forever. It is a permanent sign of my covenant with them. For in six days the LORD made heaven and earth, but he rested on the seventh day and was refreshed.

Keeping the Sabbath was serious business in the Old Testament. Failure to do so was utter rebellion against God, and the most serious consequences resulted from such a breach of the covenant. This is illustrated in the story of the man who gathered wood on the Sabbath during the wilderness wandering. After Moses and Aaron reviewed the case and sought God's will, the following answer came: "The man must be put to death! The whole community must stone him outside the camp" (Num. 15:35).

The centrality of the Sabbath in the Old Testament law is seen in the fact that it is highlighted among other laws as a sign of the covenant (Exod. 31:13, 16–17; see also Ezek. 20:12, 20).

SABBATH AND CREATION

Now that we understand the covenantal context of the Sabbath, we may return to God's instruction for observing the Sabbath as found in the fourth commandment of Exodus 20.[6] Here the motive for ceasing from work is the creation. In Genesis 1 we see the pattern articulated in God's creative work—six days of work, followed by a final day, the seventh, of rest.

Genesis 2:1–3 is especially instructive:

> So the creation of the heavens and the earth and everything in them was completed. On the seventh day, having finished his task, God rested from all his work. And God blessed the seventh day and declared it holy, because it was the day when he rested from his work of creation.

On the basis of this pattern of God's creative work and rest, the fourth commandment calls us to rest on the seventh day.

Genesis 2:1–3 does not give us additional insight into the length of the creation days, though both sides of the debate use it that way. Those who argue for the twenty-four–hour day suggest that since the Sabbath as we now observe it is twenty-four hours, the original Sabbath and, by implication, the other six days need to be understood as normal days. Such an approach does not take into account that a normal day is defined by the alternation of sunlight with darkness. The fact that the sun, moon, and stars are not created until the fourth day renders this understanding suspect.

Those who understand the days of creation as long periods of time argue that the Sabbath day is still going on. After all, once creation is done, it is done, and God continues his rest. They combine this argument with the assertion that the Hebrew word for "day" (*yom*) means a long period of time in some contexts. That is true, but only when *yom* occurs in a set formula such as "Day of the Lord."

The bottom line is that Genesis 1 and 2 do not intend to answer our questions concerning God's procedure in creation—how God created the universe. The creation accounts glorify him as Creator and remind us right away that we are creatures totally dependent upon him.

In any case, the fact that the Sabbath was, in a sense, built into creation cautions us not to hastily dismiss the Sabbath as a temporary institution. The Sabbath, along with marriage and work, are institutions established at the time God created humanity. While the pattern of creation does not make an institution or activity unchangeable for eternity,[7] it certainly is a strong argument for the continuing validity of the Sabbath as an institution.

SABBATH AND REDEMPTION

Scholars have long noted that there are minute differences between the wording of the Ten Commandments in Exodus and in Deuteronomy. Deuteronomy, after all, is the "second giving of the law." It appears that when Moses brought the law to mind in his last sermon to the Israelites before his death and their entry into the promised land, he felt the freedom to contextualize the law to their present circumstances. This, of course, resulted not in wholesale changes, but rather subtle ones. The most obvious differences are found in the fourth commandment. Among other changes, we see in Deuteronomy a new motive clause for observing the Sabbath:

> Observe the Sabbath day by keeping it holy, as the LORD your God has commanded you. Six days a week are set apart for your daily duties and regular work, but the seventh day is a day of rest dedicated to the LORD your God. On that day no one in your household may do any kind of work. This includes you, your sons and daughters, your male and female servants, your oxen and donkeys and other livestock, and any foreigners living among you. All your male and female servants

must rest as you do. Remember that you were once slaves in Egypt and that the LORD your God brought you out with amazing power and mighty deeds. That is why the LORD your God has commanded you to observe the Sabbath day. (Deut. 5:12–15)

On comparison, we can immediately see that Deuteronomy has what we might call a more social-justice orientation. There is a strong concern to see that the benefits of redemption are applied beyond the people of God to foreigners and slaves who labor in their midst. Furthermore, and more to the point, the motive for keeping the Sabbath is God's work of redemption. Israel's redemption was won by God himself, not through their own labor. God owns them and controls their destiny. Resting from work on the Sabbath is a way, first of all, to enjoy the redemption that God has won for them. Second, it is a way of giving up control and the idea that we gain in life only by working hard.

From this survey of Old Testament teaching, we can see why the Sabbath is such an important institution. It is closely connected with some of the most fundamental teachings of the Bible: creation, redemption, covenant, and law. The Sabbath was a weekly, regular setting apart of time from common, everyday work. It was a time for special sacrifices (Num. 28:9–10) and meeting for the purpose of worship (Lev. 23:3).

But how does the New Testament appropriate the Sabbath? Should God's people observe it in exactly the same way, or is all time now considered sacred? After all, we have already seen that, whereas in the Old Testament we may speak of sacred space, people, and acts, the New Testament has expanded the concept of holiness beyond these ideas. Before looking at the New Testament Sabbath, we need to consider the Old Testament teaching on extending the weekly Sabbath to a full year.

THE SABBATICAL YEAR

The weekly Sabbath found larger expression in the sabbatical year. Leviticus 25 describes a system whereby every seventh year was a Sabbath, when no field was to be planted, pruned, or harvested. Indeed, the Israelite farmer was not even permitted to store any crop that was produced naturally. Everyone could eat this food, but it could not be stored. Israel's observance of this regulation was totally a matter of trusting God. The agriculture of the area was tenuous enough normally. To actually give up a year of work and expect to eat the following year was to believe that God could and would take care of his people.

In addition to the sabbatical year, Leviticus 25 also informs us that the seventh seven-year period came with special significance.[8] This "Jubilee" year not only saw the fields lying fallow, but also was a time when property was redeemed and slaves were released. The intention was to return the land to those who originally received it from God. A family may have been forced to sell their land sometime within the fifty-year period, but it always returned to the original owners at the end. Of course, when land was purchased, its price would be set in light of the time left before the next Jubilee. It was more like leasing than selling real estate. In any case, this practice would have prohibited great inequalities between the "haves" and the "have-nots" among God's people. In addition, any Israelites who had to sell themselves into slavery in order to pay debts would, at the time of Jubilee, have their freedom again.

Thus, we can see what a picture of redemption the sabbatical year and the Jubilee year were in ancient Israel. They were outgrowths of the weekly Sabbath and required utter dependence on God. They were symbols of the rest that only God's redemption could supply.

Unfortunately, Israel rarely, if ever, actually observed

sabbatical years, according to biblical testimony. At the end of Chronicles comes this explanation for the length of the Babylonian exile: "The land finally enjoyed its Sabbath rest, lying desolate for seventy years, just as the prophet had said" (2 Chron. 36:21).

FOR FURTHER REFLECTION

1. What is your attitude toward Old Testament law?
2. If you are in the practice of observing the Sabbath now, do you also observe the Sabbath year? Why or why not?
3. How do we know that the Sabbath was such a fundamental Old Testament institution?
4. Before reading the next chapter, articulate your present attitude toward the Sabbath. Is it a day like any other day? A day of rest and refreshment? A boring day?

16

CHRIST AND SABBATH:
SACRED TIME
RECONFIGURED

B y now in our study of the priestly theology of the
Old Testament, we are sensitive to the relationship
between Christ and the Old Testament. We have
seen that Christ fulfills the concepts of sacred space, people, and acts. This pattern encourages our anticipation
that Christ will also have a relationship with the concept
of sacred time. As we will soon see, we will not be disappointed in our expectation. Both the Gospels and the
Epistles illuminate the relationship between Christ and
the Sabbath and instruct us as to God's will for our present actions.

THE GOSPELS AND THE SABBATH

The Sabbath was a time for rest and worship, so we
are not surprised to find Jesus in the synagogue on Sabbath days. In Mark, the first report of his Sabbath activities may be found in 1:21–28. He is in Capernaum where
he goes into the synagogue and begins to teach. His
teaching is met with amazement by his listeners. During

this service Jesus is confronted by an evil spirit who has possessed a man, and casting it out, Jesus further amazes those in attendance.

If this report were typical of Jesus' Sabbath activities, we could easily conclude that he did not deviate in the least from the Old Testament perspective on the Sabbath. But we don't have to read far into the Gospels before we realize that Jesus was often at odds with the religious authorities of his day concerning the proper Sabbath observance. And that raises the question of his relationship to the Old Testament institution. Does he conform in the main to Old Testament law concerning the Sabbath and just peel off the Jewish additions to that law or is there something more fundamental at work?

In Mark 2:23–28 the authorities challenge Jesus when he and his disciples pick grain in the field on the Sabbath. The Pharisees have Old Testament law on their side: harvesting was prohibited on the Sabbath (Exod. 34:21). While some readers of this account believe that Jesus' actions are not actually harvesting and therefore not a matter of the law, it is important to recall an earlier story, in Exodus 16:25–29, concerning the gathering of the manna.

Because gathering manna on the Sabbath was prohibited, a double portion was to be gathered the day before. The principle seems to be that Sabbath observance requires foresight. If one is hungry on the Sabbath, that is because one did not plan ahead. The Old Testament law, strictly observed, did not allow room for picking grain on the Sabbath to satisfy personal hunger. This passage makes it very difficult for us to argue that Jesus was simply challenging Pharisaic interpretation of the Sabbath law. His actions rather indicate a new approach to the Sabbath.

Indeed, Jesus' defense of his actions appears even more radical than his actions. He states that David and his companions broke the law when they ate the consecrated bread, which was meant only for priests.[1] So in a sense, Jesus' defense isn't that he and his disciples did not break the law; the precedent he cites is a case where the law was broken more than once. They ate consecrated bread on the Sabbath. In other words, their urgent need took precedence over the strict requirements of the law, because "the Sabbath was made to benefit people, and not people to benefit the Sabbath" (Mark 2:27).

That verse is cryptic and somewhat ambiguous, but minimally it insists that the Sabbath was not made to be a burden, but rather the occasion for the enjoyment and improvement of Christ's followers. To interpret the Sabbath in a way that brings additional burdens and restrictions and guilt on oneself or others is to clearly misunderstand the intention of the day.

Climactically, Jesus then announces himself as the ultimate interpreter of what is right or wrong on the Sabbath. This is evident in his dramatic conclusion, "I, the Son of Man, am master even of the Sabbath!" (Mark 2:28). This explains the earlier allusion to David. David was a precursor to Christ, a messianic king who foreshadowed the ultimate Messiah. If David could break the law in fulfillment of his role, how much more Christ himself?

Mark's very next story (3:1–6) sees Jesus go on the offensive. Now he essentially picks a fight with the Pharisees. He knows they are watching, and he heals a person on the Sabbath. Before he actually performs the healing, he poses a question to challenge them: "Is it legal to do good deeds on the Sabbath, or is it a day for doing harm? Is this a day to save life or to destroy it?" (v. 4). He answers his own question by healing the man, and the Pharisees can say nothing in response. This is just one of a number of Sabbath healings that Jesus performs during his earthly ministry (cf. Luke 13:10–17).

Jesus is carefully pushing the religious leaders of the day. He prods them by his actions and his words, showing them that the "master of the Sabbath"—in fact, the preeminent lawgiver and interpreter—is in their presence. Perhaps Jesus' most challenging statement on the Sabbath in the Gospels is found in John 5:17, in response to harassment from the religious authorities: "My Father never stops working, so why should I?" Their response is vicious because they recognized the danger of his comments: "So the Jewish leaders tried all the more to kill him. In addition to disobeying the Sabbath rules, he had spoken of God as his Father, thereby making himself equal with God" (v. 18).

According to the Gospels, Jesus is the one who unsettles contemporary strict observance of the Sabbath even during his lifetime. What happens after his death and resurrection? We turn now to Paul to get a post-resurrection perspective on the Sabbath.

PAUL ON CHRIST'S IMPACT ON THE SABBATH

When we turn to Paul, we see that the few times he mentions special holy days and in particular the Sabbath, he speaks in a way that announces important and significant transitions from Old Testament forms of worship to those inaugurated by the coming of Christ. He leads us to believe that it is wrong-minded to worship God in exactly the same way as was done in the Old Testament. We turn first to Galatians 4:8–12:

> Before you Gentiles knew God, you were slaves to so-called gods that do not even exist. And now that you have found God (or should I say, now that God has found you), why do you want to go back again and become slaves once more to the weak and useless spiritual powers of this world? You are trying to find favor with God by what you do or don't do on certain days or months or seasons or years. I fear for you. I am afraid that all

my hard work for you was worth nothing. Dear friends, I plead with you to live as I do in freedom from these things, for I have become like you Gentiles were—free from the law.

Surely, in this context, Paul is concerned about the Galatians being imprisoned by the law. His reference to "days" certainly includes the Sabbath, while his reference to "months or seasons or years" refers to the annual religious festivals and sabbatical years that I will describe in the following chapters. Our understanding is confirmed by Colossians 2:16: "So don't let anyone condemn you for what you eat or drink, or for not celebrating certain holy days or new-moon[2] ceremonies or Sabbaths. For these rules were only shadows of the real thing, Christ himself." Christ has fulfilled sacred time! All time is holy.

While Christ's fulfillment of the weekly Sabbath is indirectly implied by the New Testament, Christ's relationship to the yearly Sabbath and particularly the Jubilee year is clearly stated. Indeed, one day Jesus walked into the synagogue in his home town of Nazareth and read the Scripture passage for the day from Isaiah 61:1–2:

> The Spirit of the Lord is upon me,
>   for he has appointed me to preach Good
>   News to the poor.
> He has sent me to proclaim
>   that captives will be released,
>   that the blind will see,
>   that the downtrodden will be freed from their
>   oppressors,
>   and that the time of the Lord's favor has
>   come. (Luke 4:18–19)

Here Jesus applies the teaching of Isaiah 61 to himself, and this agitates the crowd. After all, the Isaiah passage was understood as anticipating the Messiah, the one who would establish the eschatological Jubilee, when the redemption would once and for all be accomplished. Jesus is the Messiah; he is the one who announces and accomplishes our final salvation. He is the Sabbath.

SUMMARY ON SABBATH

We have seen how Christ's coming has brought an end to the existence of a holy place. Now every place is holy, imbued with the presence of God. We may have fellowship with him anywhere in the cosmos. We have seen how there is no longer a special caste of people, like the priests, who are holier than anyone else. Everyone is a priest, set apart in intimate relationship to God. We have seen how there are no longer particular acts that are more sacred than others. Christ is the once-and-for-all sacrifice. We do not perform these holy acts any longer. These facts lead to a strong presumptive argument that there is no longer only a limited time that is considered holy; rather all time is fraught with the possibility of being in God's presence. This is good news! Because of Christ's fulfillment of sacred space, acts, persons, and time, we all have full access to him any place and all the time.

And doesn't the New Testament insist that we not reserve our worship of God to just one day a week? Paul, in so many words, describes and commands perpetual prayer (Phil. 1:4; 1 Thess. 5:17). True, worship in the special presence of God took place on the holy ground of the tabernacle continually, and though we know little about private devotion in the Old Testament, it is likely that individuals could pray to God from anywhere (even in the belly of a large fish [Jonah 2]); but there was something distinctive about the character of worship on the Sabbath that could not be replicated during the week, just as there was something distinctive about worship at the tabernacle/temple that could not take place at home. This changes as we turn to the New Testament.

CONTINUING OBSERVANCE?

Thus, our survey of the Sabbath has presented the following points that are, at least initially, in tension with one another:

(1) The Sabbath principle is embedded in creation, redemption, covenant, and law.

(2) On the other hand, the pattern of fulfillment would lead us to expect that Christ fulfills holy time in a similar fashion to how he fulfills holy space, actions, and people so that all time, space, actions, and people are holy. That some fundamental shift in understanding the Sabbath is involved is further confirmed by explicit statements in the Gospels and Epistles (Mark 2:23–28; 3:1–6; Luke 13:10–17; John 5:17; Gal. 4:8–12; Col. 2:16; and see Rom. 14:1, 5–6, 10 cited below).

(3) Christians are told to assemble together regularly (Heb. 10:25), and the verses that mention the time of gathering indicate that it was the first and not the last day of the week (Acts 20:7; 1 Cor. 16:2). Further, though we have seen that the New Testament teaches that there is no holy place like the tabernacle, Jesus does say that he will be with his people in a special way in corporate gatherings (Matt. 18:20; 1 Cor. 14:25).

How do we put these points together? Before I make a suggestion, let me take this opportunity to say that the combination of these truths is why there are differences among Christians, even Reformed Christians, on this matter. It is not that nonsabbatarians are faithful to Scripture and those who observe the Sabbath are adding human-made laws. It is not that sabbatarians are faithful to Scripture and nonsabbatarians just want to live a lawless life. Both viewpoints struggle with the biblical material and want to live in a manner pleasing to God. The Scriptures are clear about the heart of the gospel—that is a position argued by the Reformers against ecclesiastical obscurantism—but the doctrine of the perspicuity and sufficiency of Scripture does not claim that the Bible is crystal clear on every point of doctrine and practice.

The important aspects concerning contemporary Sabbath practice are clear. Everyone recognizes that Christ's coming brought a shift in Sabbath observance. This may be seen in the fact that the vast majority of Christians, and all Reformed Christians of whom I am aware, meet formally for worship on Sunday and not on the Sabbath instituted at creation and recognized throughout the Old Testament, namely Friday sundown until Saturday sundown.

Interestingly, though, there is no explicit biblical injunction to make this move. Of course, that is why the Adventist tradition still worships on Saturday. Sure, there are hints from the New Testament that the early church met on the first day of the week (Acts 20:7; 1 Cor. 16:2). We may even affirm good theological reasons for meeting on Sunday, the first day of the week rather than the last, now that Christ has come. Further, if Christ was raised on what we call Sunday, then meeting on that day would be a perpetual reminder of that central redemptive act. But, let me underline again that these are not expressly scriptural justifications.

Even though we do not have an explicit command to change the day, I think that the church is more than justified to meet on Sunday rather than Friday evening or Saturday. After all, Christ has made every day holy, though there is also the command to meet together in formal worship of God. We are not to forsake the assembly of the saints (Heb. 10:25). The early church met regularly in worship and fellowship. What better day to meet than Sunday? All days are holy, but there is a need for a special day. The early Christians met on Sunday.

We cannot think of Sunday as a uniquely holy day, but it is a special day. An analogy may be drawn with the other three areas of place, action, and people. There is no longer an exclusive holy place like the tabernacle or temple, but, as mentioned above, Jesus did say he would be with a gathering of three or more of his people in a special way (Matt. 18:20). There are no more specifically holy acts like sacrifices, but there are special acts like baptism and the Lord's Supper. All eating is to be done for the glory of God, but there is indeed something special about taking communion. All redeemed people are holy, and all legitimate vocations are holy and may be used by God, but Paul does call on us to pay "double honor" to those who are engaged in ministry (1 Tim. 4:17).

Thus, perhaps the category of a special day stripped of the ceremonial qualities of the Old Testament may apply to Sunday. The structure of the week is built into the world as God created it (Gen. 1:1–2:4). It is in keeping with the Sabbath principle to set aside one day to give our focused attention to the worship of God. It would be wrong to meet on a less frequent basis and irregular to meet on a different day than Sunday, given the indications within the New Testament and the long history of church tradition.

Even so, I leave this important and controversial subject with a final quotation from Paul that demands our attention. The apostle implicitly admits that there can be legitimate disagreements over this complex issue and that we must continue to love one another in spite of this. If we all learn only this lesson, then we will have learned much.

Accept Christians who are weak in faith, and don't argue with them about what they think is right or wrong. . . . In the same way, some think one day is more holy than another day, while others think every day is alike. Each person should have a personal conviction about this matter. Those who have a special day for worshiping the Lord are trying to honor him. . . .

Why do you condemn another Christian? Why do you look down on another Christian? (Rom. 14:1, 5–6, 10)

Paul's final admonition is for us not to judge each other in our practices in these and other areas. Those who believe that Sunday is the Sabbath should be allowed to follow their conscience, and those who are convinced otherwise should be able to do the same.

THE FINAL SABBATH: ESCHATOLOGICAL SACRED TIME

Even so, there is more to say. The author of Hebrews uses Sabbath imagery to describe the future blessings of heaven. Whether we commemorate a day of rest on the first, seventh, or another day, there is more yet to come.

God's promise of entering his place of rest still stands. . . . For this Good News—that God has prepared a place of rest—has been announced to us just as it was to them. . . . So there is a special rest still waiting for the people of God. . . . Let us do our best to enter that place of rest. For anyone who disobeys God, as the people of Israel did, will fall. (Heb. 4:1–2, 9, 11)

We should anticipate a final Sabbath, a day of ultimate redemption and rest in God. A trumpet will announce the day of Christ's return that will initiate this time.[3]

FOR FURTHER REFLECTION

1. Reflect on the answer you gave to question 3 at the end of chapter 15. Now that you have thought about the New Testament passages presented in this chapter, have your views changed or stayed the same?
2. In what ways is heaven going to be like the final Sabbath?

I7

THE *HAGGIM*
(PILGRIMAGE FESTIVALS):
MORE ON SACRED TIME

◈

We now turn our attention from the weekly and annual Sabbaths to yearly celebrations. In this chapter, we will describe and explore the three *Haggim*, that is, pilgrimage festivals. These were the three times each year that every Israelite male was to travel to Jerusalem and offer sacrifices. This pilgrimage is what binds these three festivals together. By presenting them together in this chapter, we are not following the chronological sequence of the year. If we were, both Trumpets and Atonement would be treated just before Tabernacles. These three festivals are also united in that they commemorated both agricultural and redemptive historical milestones.

THE PASSOVER AND THE FESTIVAL
OF UNLEAVENED BREAD

Passover and Exodus

According to biblical tradition, the Passover festival originated in the events surrounding the rescue of Israel from Egypt, in other words the Exodus. The Exodus was a pivotal event in the history of the Old Testament people of God. Hundred of years before, the Israelites' forebears—Jacob, Joseph, and their families—had left the promised land, where they were still sojourners, and gone to Egypt to seek food in the midst of a devastating famine. As the generations passed and the Israelite people became more numerous, the Egyptians worried that they might be outnumbered and their dominance might be threatened. Indeed, though the exact timing in relationship to Israelite history is unclear and debated, there was a Semitic incursion into Egypt, and the Hyksos had actually reigned over Egypt for a significant period of time (ca. 1640–1534 B.C.) before they were forcibly removed by Kamose and his brother Ahmose, who regained the kingship for native Egyptians.

To complicate matters a bit further, we cannot be dogmatic about the exact date of the Exodus. The book of Exodus itself keeps this matter shrouded by not naming the Egyptian kings of this time. Moses may well have been following the Egyptian practice of not honoring one's enemies by naming them, but it leaves later readers with some ambiguity over when the events of the Exodus, conquest, and settlement took place.

This is not the time to enter into a lengthy discussion of these issues. That would involve interpreting biblical texts like 1 Kings 6:1, which seems so clear on the surface, but then invites questions as to whether the number should be taken in a strictly literal sense or is symbolic for twelve generations of forty years each. If the latter, the argument runs,[1] then the literal time period is not 480 years but rather about three hundred years. Thus, we are left with the question of whether the Exodus took place in the fifteenth century or the thirteenth century B.C.[2]

However, for our purposes, it suffices to point out that whether the Exodus took place in the fifteenth century or a century or so later, it was a time of liberation, as well as an awesome display of God's power. God did not rescue his people in a flash. God hardened pharaoh's heart so that he might demonstrate to Egypt, as well as his own people, his great power. So the first few chapters of Exodus (7–11) narrate a series of signs and plagues by which God progressively showed his superiority over the mighty Egyptians. In fact, the biblical text understands the plagues as a fight between the true God, Yahweh, and the Egyptian gods, who are false and pretenders. We see this explicitly in regard to the last plague, the one most relevant to the Passover celebration, namely the plague on the first-born of Egypt: "On that night I will pass through the land of Egypt and kill all the firstborn sons and firstborn male animals in the land of Egypt. I will execute judgment against all the gods of Egypt, for I am the LORD!" (Exod. 12:12). It is with this final, destructive plague that the pharaoh finally gave in and allowed the Israelites to leave Egypt. Because it was such a pivotal moment, the Israelites were told to celebrate a festival annually to commemorate the events.

Indeed, it is interesting to note how the historic, first-occasion Passover is narrated in Exodus 12–13.[3] It is not told merely as a historical memorial, but rather it comes to us in the form of instructions for how to observe the meal and the broader festival, not only that special first night, but for years and years to come.

Ritual Instructions

In anticipation of the death of the first-born of Egypt, Israel was to celebrate a festival whose name in Hebrew is *pesah*. The word *pesah* is of uncertain origins, but its origins are no more relevant than the etymologies of other words. What is really important is how the word is used in the context of this festival. In this connection, we should pay close attention to 12:23, which says that the Lord would "pass over"[4] the doors of the Israelites with the result that the first born in those houses would not die. How would the angel of death determine which houses to enter and do his work and which to "pass over"? The answer is given in the ritual that Moses is told to command the Israelites to follow.

On the tenth day of the first month (Nisan, which today is March/April) faithful Israelite households were to select a lamb (the Hebrew term also could be a goat) for sacrifice. The animal was to be only one year old and without defect. Notice that this sacred festival was the only one where heads of households were told to perform the sacrifice. This, of course, is because it was established before the ordination of the priests. It may be that later the priests took over this function, but we have here the precedent for the celebration of the Passover in Jewish homes today with no official priest on hand.

Four days later, on the fourteenth of the month of Nisan, the sacrificial animals were to be sacrificed. The blood was to be drained and smeared on the doorframes of their houses. It is an error to think of this blood as magical. It was rather symbolic of death, and this sacrifice, as explained in part two, on sacrifices, was an atoning sacrifice. The animal stood in the place of the occupants, particularly the first-born occupants of the house. As T. D. Alexander points out, "The sacrifice of the animal atones for the sin of the people, the blood smeared on the door-posts purifies those within, and the eating of the sacrificial meat consecrates those who consume it. By participating in the Passover ritual the people sanctify themselves as a nation holy to God (cf. 19:6)."[5]

The night on which the sacrifice took place was the same night that the meal was to be eaten. The Passover meal was the center of the ritual. According to Exodus 12:8 the meat was to be accompanied by a vegetable, namely bitter herbs, and a grain, bread without yeast (the significance of which will be pointed out later). Further instructions are given, concerning the mode of cooking the animal, as well as the requirement that any meat left over on the next day must be burned and not eaten. After all, it had a consecrated purpose. To use it for next day's lunch, a common purpose, would have been sacrilegious.

At the conclusion of Exodus 12 (vv. 43–51) additional regulations are brought to our attention. Significant for later biblical theological connections is the command not to break the bones of the sacrificial animal. These verses also delimit the celebration of the festival to Israelites and their slaves. Hired slaves and foreigners were not permitted to participate. Presumably, the slaves were considered a part of the household in a way that hired servants were not.

The Passover and the Song of Songs

At first glance, it is surprising that the Song is in the scroll (the Megilloth) associated with the Passover. The Song is a love poem, or anthology of love poems, that celebrates the divinely instituted relationship between a man and a woman. However, early interpretations rejected what they thought was an unworthy interpretation for the divine Scriptures and asserted an allegorical approach. This approach to the Song was arbitrary in its interpretation, but started with the reasonable assumption that God was the man and Israel was the woman who were romantically involved. Most likely the connection between the Song and the Exodus and thus the Passover came as a result of this faulty interpretation. When the woman, who is Israel, calls to the man, namely God, to bring her into his bedroom at the start of the book (Song 1:2–4), this was interpreted to mean that Israel was asking God to bring her out of Egypt and into the promised land.

Even though this reasoning is faulty, it is not completely out of line to think of the Song and the Passover as related. After all, throughout the Bible, God and Israel and, later, God and the church are metaphorically described as married. There is, in other words, a theological dimension to the Song.[6]

The Relationship between the Passover and Unleavened Bread

Scholars debate over the original relationship between the Passover and the Feast of Unleavened Bread, with many of them weighing in on the side of their originally separate origins. The feeling is that Unleavened Bread was a springtime agricultural festival that was later given redemptive-historical meaning and attached to the Exodus idea. While that is possible—there is certainly nothing objectionable about an earlier agricultural festival being given a new meaning—what is clear is that Passover and Unleavened Bread are united in every biblical text.[7] Supposed subtle indications of their separate beginnings aside, there is good reason to believe that Unleavened Bread was very appropriate to the Passover celebration. After all, according to the biblical text, the Israelites hurried out of Egypt, so much so that they did not wait to add leaven and allow their bread for the journey to rise (Exod. 12:34; 13:3).

This part of the festival lasted seven days, beginning with the Passover meal. Thus, from the time the animal was initially chosen to the end of the Feast of Unleavened Bread was a period of eleven days, from the tenth of Nisan until the twenty-first. The Passover and the accompanying Festival of Unleavened Bread were accordingly celebrations of redemption marked with hope. These characteristics make it amenable to association with a later climactic redemption that has brought hope to the world.

New Testament Connections

We have already anticipated the deep connections between the Passover and Jesus Christ when we explored the connection between the Passover sacrifice and Christ's sacrifice. According to 1 Corinthians 5:7, "Christ, our Passover lamb, has been sacrificed for us." In the verse that follows, Paul plays with the connection between the Passover and bread without yeast: "So let us celebrate the festival, not by eating the old bread of wickedness and evil, but by eating the new bread of purity and truth" (v. 8). As the NLT footnote indicates, the first bread, the symbol of wickedness, is bread with yeast, according to the Greek, and the bread that represents purity and truth is the bread without the yeast.

We do not need to repeat the extensive parallels between Jesus' life and the events of the Exodus (for review, see pp. 113–15). But they certainly intend to drive home the idea that Jesus is the fulfillment of the Passover lamb. He was crucified on the eve of the Passover, and the gospel of John adds the significant note that the soldiers did not break his legs—though that was the usual practice in a Roman crucifixion—in keeping with the practice of leaving the Passover sacrifice's legs intact (see John 19:31–37).

THE FESTIVAL OF WEEKS (PENTECOST)

The Festival of Weeks was the second *hag* or pilgrimage festival of the year where all Israelite men were required to appear before the Lord in Jerusalem (Deut. 16:16). These pilgrims were to bring gifts to the Lord at this time.

The festival goes by different names. Often it is referred to as the Festival of Harvest, since it was integrally connected to the agricultural cycle. The date of the festival corresponded to the appearance of the first grain harvested in the year. Leviticus 23:9–14 narrates a ritual involving the "firstfruits" of the harvest. Hartley informs us that, though there are four different traditions concerning when this day would appear in the calendar, all four closely connect it to a Sabbath either during or after the Feast of Unleavened Bread.[8] The first bit of grain was to be waved before the Lord on the day after the Sabbath on which it was brought. This symbolically acknowledged that the harvest comes from God. The wave offering was accompanied by the sacrifice of a lamb along with a grain offering and a drink offering.

It was at the point of this firstfruit offering that the Israelites were to count off seven weeks. Specifically, on the day after the seventh Sabbath, the fiftieth day, the people were to offer up an offering that commemorated the grain harvest. Thus this festival was also known as the Feast of Weeks, described in Leviticus 23:15–22.

The offering is described in the sacrificial list found in Numbers 28:26–31:[9]

> On the first day of the Festival of Harvest, when you present the first of your new grain to the LORD, you must call a holy assembly of the people. None of your regular work may be done on that day. A special whole burnt offering will be offered that day, very pleasing to the LORD. It will consist of two young bulls, one ram, and seven one-year-old male lambs. These will be accompanied by grain offerings of choice flour mixed with olive oil—five quarts with each bull, three quarts with the ram, and two quarts with each of the seven lambs. Also, offer one male goat to make atonement for yourselves. These special burnt offerings, along with their drink offerings, are in addition to the regular daily burnt offering and its accompanying grain offering. Be sure that all the animals you sacrifice have no physical defects.

Pentecost, with its association with the grain harvest, was a day of great joy and celebration. Work ceased for the occasion, and a sacred assembly was held, presumably to offer thanks for the harvest before God. The offerings were large for this festival, probably because of the abundance that the people enjoyed in connection with the harvest. Furthermore, it is interesting to note the special concern expressed toward the poor and foreigners (Lev. 23:22).

New Testament Connections

Unlike Passover and Tabernacles (below), this festival is not connected in the Old Testament to a redemptive event like the Exodus. It is connected exclusively to the agricultural cycle. It is in the New Testament that we have an association between this Israelite/Jewish festival and an act of God's redemption in history. We immediately recognize this when we realize that the festival goes by yet another name in the New Testament, one familiar to modern Christian readers. Jewish people in the first century referred to this festival as Pentecost, formed from the Greek word "fifty," which refers to the fifty-day period after the offering of the first bit of grain. And Pentecost is immediately recognized as the day when, in a very important sense, the church was founded.

The story appears in Acts 2 and begins with the announcement that the following events took place on Pentecost, fifty days after Passover, which, we have already observed, was the festival before which Christ was crucified. As one of the three *haggim* or pilgrimage festivals, Pentecost filled Jerusalem with people from all around the world. Jewish people not only from Palestine but also from the diaspora had come to offer sacrifices at the temple. Acts 2:9–11 lists "Parthians, Medes, Elamites, people from Mesopotamia, Judea, Cappodocia, Pontus, the province of Asia, Phrygia, Pamphylia, Egypt, and the areas of Libya toward Cyrene, visitors from Rome (both Jews and converts to Judaism), Cretans, and Arabians." This impressive list represents the nations of the world.

Those who already believed in Jesus were meeting together when suddenly there was a huge sound like a rushing wind, and flames that looked like tongues appeared on each of them. One does not read long in the Old Testament before encountering similar, though perhaps not identical, themes. God often appeared in the Old Testament in the form of a whirlwind (think of Job 38:1) or fire (think of the burning bush in Exod. 3). Indeed, God was appearing here in the form of the Holy Spirit, who filled them and caused them to speak in other languages.

This was not the "unknown language" that many people today exclusively identify with "tongues," rather these were the languages of the foreign visitors to Jerusalem. All of a sudden the followers of God were speaking Elamite, Arabic, Phrygian, Greek, Latin, and all the other languages of the world. What we have here is a reversal of Genesis 11 and the Tower of Babel episode. There, because of the sin of humanity—in particular, an attempt to reach heaven by mere human power—God confused the speech of humanity. Before that time there was one language, but afterward there were many, so that the different language groups could not immediately understand each other. Just after that, however, God's redemptive plan began to work through one family and one nation (Gen. 12:1–3). Here in Acts 2, Christ's followers were not hindered by multiple languages. Babel was now reversed, at least temporarily for symbolic purposes, so that the gospel message might get out.

Note too that Peter understood the events of this day to be in accordance with Joel 2:28–32:

> In the last days, God said,
>   I will pour out my Spirit upon all people.
> Your sons and daughters will prophesy,
>   your young men will see visions,
>   and your old men will dream dreams.

In those days I will pour out my Spirit
upon all my servants, men and women alike,
and they will prophesy.
And I will cause wonders in the heavens above
and signs on the earth below—
blood and fire and clouds of smoke.
The sun will be turned into darkness,
and the moon will turn bloodred,
before that great and glorious day of the Lord
arrives.
And anyone who calls on the name of the Lord
will be saved. (Acts 2:17–21)

Pentecost had many of the earmarks of the Day of the Lord. More was to come, to be sure, but most particularly here, we see that the Spirit was poured out on both genders, all social classes, and all ages. Everyone who follows Christ is a prophet, that is, one whom God has commissioned to speak the gospel to the nations. Moses' prayer in Numbers 11:29 has been answered in a full and rich sense: "I wish that all the LORD's people were prophets, and that the LORD would put his Spirit upon them all!"

How utterly appropriate for the birth of the church! The gospel of Matthew ends with Jesus' instruction to reach out to the nations:

I have been given complete authority in heaven and on earth. Therefore, go and make disciples of all the nations, baptizing them in the name of the Father and the Son and the Holy Spirit. Teach these new disciples to obey all the commands I have given to you. And be sure of this: I am with you always, even to the end of the age. (28:18–20)

The ability to speak in other languages during this Pentecost was not gratuitous; it gave Christians the possibility of spreading the good news to representatives of the whole world. On that day, there were 120 believers in the upper room who were filled with the Spirit. By the end of the day, there were three thousand believers—a sign of things to come!

The church was born on this day. Jesus' act of redemption was completely accomplished. He was crucified, was raised, and ascended into heaven. As he had promised, he now had sent the Holy Spirit. Indeed, we should note that when Peter actually preached on this Pentecost, the emphasis was not on the miraculous events induced by the Spirit, as exciting and important as they were, but rather on Christ himself.

Is it coincidental that the church was founded on Pentecost? Hardly. Remember that this festival was a harvest festival. Many places in the New Testament speak of the fruits of preaching the gospel as a harvest. The many converts on Pentecost, thus, were the firstfruits of the harvest of people who would turn to Christ, thanks to the power of the Holy Spirit.

THE FESTIVAL OF TABERNACLES

The agricultural "roots" of at least some of the Old Testament festivals are clearly seen in the third annual *hag* (pilgrimage) of the year. The origin of the festival may be seen in part by the multiple names attached to it. We know it both as the Festival of Ingathering and as the Festival of Tabernacles or Booths (*sukkot*).

The timing was related to its importance for the agricultural cycle. It took place five days after the Day of Atonement. In other words it began on the fifteenth day of the seventh month (Tishri). That was equivalent to mid-October in our calendar and coincided with the final efforts at harvesting the crops. In Deuteronomy 16 we learn that the festival took place after the grain was threshed and the grapes were pressed. The work was done, and so the celebration could begin. As we might imagine in that agricultural society, the act of final harvest was a time of great rejoicing and celebration. It was a time of abundance, and so thanks was due to the one—namely the LORD—who had given these wonderful gifts of the earth. Deuteronomy 16:14 says it clearly when it describes the festival as a "happy time of rejoicing with your family, with your servants, and with the Levites, foreigners, orphans, and widows."

However, as with all the festivals that were rooted in the agricultural cycle, the Festival of Tabernacles was also given great redemptive-historical significance. One of the rituals of this particular festival was that each Israelite family was to construct a makeshift booth, or temporary living structure, out of the branches and leaves of trees. Indeed, in Leviticus 23:42–43 the Israelites are told to live in these booths for the duration of the festival in order to "remind each new generation of Israelites that their ancestors had to live in shelters when I rescued them from the land of Egypt. I, the LORD, am your God."

Thus, Leviticus connects the festival with the Exodus–wilderness-wanderings complex of God's redemption. If the Israelites ever did actually live in these booths, it would certainly have reminded them of God's goodness in getting them out of the wilderness and established in the promised land! But there are indications, which I will mention below, that this ceremony was rarely observed during the long period of the Old Testament.

In any case, the festival, beginning on the fifteenth day of the seventh month, lasted seven days, after which was a concluding ceremony on the eighth day. The opening day and the post-festival eighth day involved the same number of sacrifices and were each called a "sacred assembly," requiring the cessation of all work. But the seven days of the festival involved an astonishing number of sacrifices, as indicated by the list in Numbers

29:12–40. The sacrifices for each day are enumerated there. Each day young bulls, two rams, and fourteen one-year-old male lambs were offered. With these were also offered a *minhah* and a drink offering. Finally, a male goat was offered as a *hattat*. With this was the regular daily *'olah* (burnt offering), as well as its accompanying grain offering and drink offering.

The sacrifice of young bulls was the one offering that varied in number from day to day. On the first day, thirteen young bulls were offered; on the second, twelve; on the third, eleven; all the way down to the seventh day, when only seven young bulls were offered! Unfortunately, no good reasons are given for this, and the speculations are not at all convincing.

The total number of sacrifices offered at this festival was more than any other, and for this reason Tabernacles is sometimes simply called "the Feast" or "the Festival." Numbers 29 supplies some figures. During the first seven days of the festival the totals were, not surprisingly, connected to the number seven, which signifies completion or fulfillment. The total number of young bulls was seventy; the total number of rams was fourteen; the total number of lambs was ninety-eight, which is fourteen times seven. On the eighth-day assembly, after the festival was completed, there were seven lambs, one bull, one ram, and one goat, for a total of ten. The total number of animal sacrifices on these eight days was 192, and this excludes the regular daily sacrifices and the nonanimal sacrifices.

New Testament Connections

The above portrait of the Festival of the Tabernacles is derived from the Pentateuch. By the time of Nehemiah (see 8:13–18), the community of Israel hadn't observed this festival since the days of Joshua, centuries before! It had been forgotten and was re-instituted during Nehemiah's life in the second half of the fifth century B.C.

By the time of the New Testament, it was being observed again. In John 7, Jesus' brothers wanted him to go to the Festival of Shelters in order to publicly display his miracles. He told them he would not go, but he did anyway without their knowledge. By the first century, we know that a ritual visit to the Pool of Siloam was included in the festivities. Water was taken from the pool and poured out as an offering to the Lord. Many biblical scholars believe that this ritual was behind Jesus' comments about living water on the last day of the festival (John 7:37-39).

Continuing biblical theological significance is more likely to be found in the festival's connection with the Exodus and wilderness wandering events. Thus, my comments above (pp. 113-15) are relevant to the connection between Christ and the celebration of this festival.

FOR FURTHER REFLECTION

1. Why don't we observe these festivals today?
2. Even if we do not observe these festivals today, are there any principles in them that inform our present worship?
3. Can a nonagricultural society draw any lasting principles from agricultural festivals?

18

FESTIVALS OF TRUMPETS AND THE DAY OF ATONEMENT: VERY SPECIAL SACRED TIMES

❖❖❖

The Festival of Trumpets and the Day of Atonement were not connected with the agricultural cycle as the three festivals described in the previous chapter were. Neither were they *haggim*, or pilgrimage festivals. The Day of Atonement had the greater significance of the two festivals treated in this chapter. Indeed, it may have grown in significance as time went on.

THE FESTIVAL OF TRUMPETS

The Festival of Trumpets announced the onset of the seventh month of the year, the month with the largest concentration of festivals. It is mentioned in Leviticus 23:23–25 and Numbers 29:1–6, the latter text listing the sacrifices associated with the day, and the former text giving us a rather minimal description of the significance of the day. In the first place, it was a day of rest from work and a day on which there was to be a sacred assembly to worship God.

But what was the significance of the day, and what

was the purpose of the trumpets? We are left to infer the answers to these questions since Scripture is not explicit. The timing of this festival is likely significant. It was the first day of the seventh month. This month was the most holy month in that, besides Trumpets, there were two other important festivals in the seventh month: the Day of Atonement and the Festival of Tabernacles. Thus, the first day announced the onset of a particularly consecrated month. Perhaps this month was singled out in this way because it was at the end of the agricultural cycle and there was much to celebrate, as well as additional time to express corporate joy, since the bulk of the work of the year was done.[1]

The word used to designate the trumpets in Leviticus 23 and Numbers 29 is the noun *teru'a*, which in the context means "blaring." It is unclear, and probably insignificant, whether the specific instrument was a *shopar* (ram's horn) or a *hatsotsera* (a metallic instrument).[2] We will simply use the English term "trumpet" to cover both possibilities. Both instruments were used as signal instruments announcing an arrival of some sort.

In Scripture, trumpets often announce the presence of God. We see this in Exodus 19 where God makes his presence known on Mount Sinai. Since this appearance was also accompanied by lightning and thunder, it leads us to wonder whether the trumpet sound was a human replication of the thunder. Another relevant and notable instance of the trumpet announcing the presence of God, this time as divine warrior, was at the battle of Jericho, in particular on the last days, as a prelude to the collapse of the walls of that city (Josh. 6:5, 16).

THE DAY OF ATONEMENT

Earlier we explored the account of the ordination of Aaron and his sons to the priesthood, found in Leviticus 8.[3]

Leviticus 9 narrates the beginning of their priestly work. Sadly, the tenth chapter describes the sin of two of Aaron's sons, Nadab and Abihu. They offered illegitimate fire in the presence of the Lord. While there is considerable room for debate over the precise nature of the fire, there is no doubt why it brought God's swift and terrible punishment: "They disobeyed the LORD by burning before him a different kind of fire than he had commanded" (Lev. 10:1). We see here that the priests could sin and need atonement, and that their actions ritually polluted the sacred space of the tabernacle itself.

I preface our discussion of the Day of Atonement with a reminder of the priests' sin because Leviticus 16, which contains God's instructions for this ritual, roots the origin of this ritual in that sin. The sin of Nadab and Abihu elicits another warning to Aaron to be particularly careful in God's presence. He is reminded that if he is negligent and goes into God's presence at the wrong time, he will die (16:2). He is told that he may enter the Holy of Holies, the back third of the tabernacle, only once a year and for a special purpose—the annual purgation of the sanctuary, which involves sacrifices for the atonement of the priests' sins, as well as the transgressions of the people.

The bulk of Leviticus 16 describes the ritual, and it is both interesting and symbolically rich. At first the text focuses on Aaron himself. He was the one who went into the Holy of Holies; he needed to be ritually prepared, and sacrifices were needed to cover his sins before he entered the presence of God. He would begin with an investiture and lustration ritual. He was to remove his ornate priestly garments[4] and put on simpler linen garments. The day was to be characterized by abstinence—resting, fasting, and simple clothes. He also would bring two animals for sacrifice for himself and his family. A young bull would be sacrificed for a sin offering, and a ram for a whole burnt offering.

Indeed, as our description will reveal, the emphasis

of the ritual was on purgation of sin, and the sin offering (*hattat*) was the most appropriate sacrifice for this purpose. The people of Israel themselves also would bring two animals on their behalf, two goats. As the text goes on to explain, one of these goats would be sacrificed, and the other would be driven into the wilderness for reasons that I will give momentarily. Aaron would decide by casting the sacred lot which animal would die and which would be driven into the wilderness.

Having ritually prepared himself and all the requisite sacrifices, Aaron would begin by sacrificing the bull as a sin offering in accordance with Leviticus 4:3–21. He then would begin his journey into the heart of the tabernacle. We need to remember that to penetrate this far into sacred space was not taken lightly. Only the high priest could do it, and only once a year. Later rabbinic prescriptions say that the high priest could only go with a rope tied around his waist. Another priest in the courtyard would hold on to the other end of the robe. As long as the people outside heard the tinkling of the bells worn on the fringe of the priest's robe, everything was fine. However, if the bells stopped for an appreciable length of time, then they knew that the priest had met his end in the tent, and they were to drag the body out by the rope. There is no record of this actually happening, but the story reminds us of the great seriousness of this ritual.

The high priest's journey into and through the tabernacle complex had three stops, and at each location he would perform a purgative ritual. He would start with the most holy spot, namely the Holy of Holies. Once there the priest would take the incense that he had brought into this innermost shrine and burn it on coals so that it created a large cloud. He then would take the bull's blood and sprinkle it on the front of the atonement cover atop the ark of the covenant. He would put more of the bull's blood on his finger and sprinkle the blood seven times on the ark. We may picture the priest wagging his finger toward the ark with the blood flying onto the ark, as well as the floor. This perhaps signified the purification not only of the structure but also of the inner space, which would be considered holy.

The blood of the bull was to cover his sin and the sin of his family. Next he would take the blood of the slaughtered goat of the people and perform the same ritual acts in the Holy of Holies. Thus, there were two sacrifices at this first stop, one for his priestly sins and one for the sins of the people.

The interpretation of Leviticus 16:16 is disputed. Some (as I) understand the passage to indicate that Aaron was to repeat these two offerings on behalf of himself and the people in the room outside the Most Holy Place. The meaning is a little clearer in the NIV than in the NLT:

> In this way he will make atonement for the Most Holy Place because of the uncleanness and rebellion of the Israelites, whatever their sins have been. He is to do the same for the Tent of Meeting, which is among them in the midst of their uncleanness.

The suggested interpretation understands the first sentence to summarize the first stop of Aaron's ritual journey (in the Holy of Holies) and the second sentence to say that the room outside the Most Holy Place (the second stop) was similarly purged. The further suggestion is that it was specifically the incense altar that was sprinkled with blood.

Then finally Aaron was to move to the outside of the tabernacle proper and perform the blood-sprinkling in yet a third place, this time toward the great bronze altar of sacrifice in the courtyard. According to this understanding of the text, each of the major spatial components of the tabernacle complex would be purged of the effects of the priest's and people's sins.

But this was not the end of the ritual. The most interesting was yet to come.

After Aaron was done with the blood-sprinkling ritual, he would take the living goat known as the scapegoat. Literally, this goat is said to be "for Azazel." Scholars are perplexed over the meaning of this phrase in this context. Elsewhere, specifically in the intertestamental book Enoch (8:1; 9:6; 10:4–8), it is a name for a demon. Leviticus 16:8 reads literally that one goat is "for Yahweh" and the other is "for Azazel." This could indicate that the community's sins were being driven from a holy to an unclean place. Other scholars feel that Azazel was the name of a wilderness location, but this would not explain why the Hebrew says "for Azazel." Whatever the right explanation, we are left in no doubt as to the function and consequences of the ritual action; it was clearly an act of substitution for the purpose of cleansing and atonement.

We have seen in connection with certain sacrificial rituals that the laying on of hands was symbolic of the substitution of the animal for the unclean person or sinner. Aaron laid hands on the head of the goat and then drove the goat into the wilderness, presumably never to be heard from again. Aaron did not leave the sacred precinct to perform this action. Another man is said to have taken the goat out to the wilderness and released it, after which he was to cleanse his clothes and bathe before returning to the camp. The same was true for the one who took the remnants of the other sacrificial animals of the ritual. These remains were taken outside the camp by yet another individual and burned. That person too had to bathe and wash his clothes.

The ritual was extremely important for Israel. Leviticus 16:30 summarizes its effect: "On this day, atonement will be made for you, and you will be cleansed from all your sins in the LORD's presence."

The day chosen for this celebration was the tenth day of the seventh month of the year, known as Tishri. This day falls in September or October on our calendar.

Today, the nation of Israel and Jews around the world recognize the Day of Atonement (Yom Kippur) as New Year's Day. It is likely that a text like Leviticus 25:9 already connects New Year's and Yom Kippur.

New Testament Connections

The book of Acts mentions the Day of Atonement as "the Fast" (Acts 27:9 NIV). But far more theologically significant is the fact that the Day of Atonement provides the background to Hebrews 6–9. We have had occasion to refer to this section of Scripture in the preceding three parts of this book. Here I simply want to point out that Christ's act of atonement is seen as a final, once-and-for-all entering of the real Holy of Holies, namely heaven itself.

> For Christ has entered into heaven itself to appear now before God as our Advocate. He did not go into the earthly place of worship, for that was merely a copy of the real Temple in heaven. Nor did he enter heaven to offer himself again and again, like the earthly high priest who enters the Most Holy Place year after year to offer the blood of an animal. If that had been necessary, he would have had to die again and again, ever since the world began. But no! He came once for all time, at the end of the age, to remove the power of sin forever by his sacrificial death for us. (Heb. 9:24–26)

By doing this, Christ fulfilled the Day of Atonement, and Christians feel that no other atoning act is necessary, and so the rituals surrounding this Day are no longer observed.

FOR FURTHER REFLECTION

1. How do we find and express atonement today?
2. What is the significance of Christ's performing the ritual "once and for all" in heaven?

19

PURIM: LATECOMER
TO SACRED TIME

All of the sacred times described thus far are established in the first five books of the Bible, the Pentateuch. They celebrated either God's redemptive acts or his provision of crops—in a few cases, both. The redemptive acts connected to festivals such as Passover and Tabernacles had to do with the establishment of Israel as a nation. But there is one more festival that the Old Testament establishes, and that is Purim.

HISTORICAL PROVIDENCE AND PURIM

To find out about Purim we turn to one of the latest books of the Old Testament, the book of Esther. Here we have one of the most intriguing stories in the Bible. The setting is Susa, the capital of the great kingdom of Persia. The king is Ahasuerus, also known in history by his Greek name Xerxes, who ruled from 486 until 465 B.C. Thus, the events recorded in Esther occurred between the first return after the Babylonian captivity under the leadership of Sheshbazzar and Zerubbabel and the later work of Ezra and Nehemiah.

The book of Esther concerns a time when the Jewish

people were threatened with extinction. Haman, an Agagite and the Persian prime minister (Esth. 3:1), hated Mordecai, a Jewish man identified as a son of Kish, who had achieved some level of prominence in the Persian court but refused to bow to Haman. And so Haman plotted the demise not only of Mordecai but of all the Jews in the empire. He convinced the king to allow the genocide of the Jewish people. By throwing lots (*purim*) a date was determined when they would die—nearly a year in the future, specifically March 7 (Esth. 3:7).

Before this arrangement was made, however, the book tells us that two significant events already took place. First, Esther became Ahasuerus's queen. The former queen, Vashti, had offended the king and needed to be replaced. And so the king held a contest in which he "tried out" a number of women to see whom he would want. Esther won and became queen, though she had not revealed her Jewish identity to the king. Second, Mordecai was in the right place at the right time in order to foil a plot to assassinate Ahasuerus. (Both these stories are found in Esther 1–2.)

With these events in the background, Mordecai learned of Haman's plot and urged Esther to appeal to the king. At first, Esther resisted helping, but then realizing that her life was also on the line, she agreed to act.

The story of the Jewish people's redemption at this time is one of seeming coincidences and ironic reversals. *It just so happened* (as if by chance) that, like Mordecai, Esther was in the right place at the right time. *It just so happened* that the king had a sleepless night and, when his advisors read him to sleep from the historical records, he was reminded of Mordecai's act of saving his life. *It just so happened* that when Ahasuerus decided to honor Mordecai for this act, the self-serving Haman walked in and suggested a form of public honor he thought he himself deserved, but the king directed Haman to parade Mordecai through town, sing his praise, and thereby pay that very honor to Mordecai, Haman's enemy. *It just so happened* that Haman's gallows, built to hang Mordecai, were ready and available when Esther told Ahasuerus of Haman's treachery, so that Haman would die there instead of Mordecai.

Nonetheless, there was one problem remaining. It was a well-known fact that not even Persian kings were above the law. Even though Ahasuerus was the one who decreed the day when the Jewish people would be destroyed, he could not reverse his edict. Therefore he gave another edict: that the Jewish people could defend themselves against their enemies. As a result, "the Jews went ahead on the appointed day and struck down their enemies with the sword. They killed and annihilated their enemies and did as they pleased with those who hated them" (Esth. 9:5). A great victory was won that day.

Close analysis reveals that this victory had more significance than a surface reading demonstrates. I have already mentioned that Haman was a descendant of Agag and that Mordecai was a descendant of Kish. For those who know their Old Testament history well, this brings to mind an age-old conflict going back to Exodus 17:8–16. While in the wilderness, Israel was attacked by the Amalekites. Under Moses' leadership, the Israelites prevailed, but on that occasion God instructed Moses, "Write this down as a permanent record, and announce it to Joshua: I will blot out every trace of Amalek from under heaven" (v. 14). This point is reemphasized in Deuteronomy 25:17–19 where God says, "You are to destroy the Amalekites and erase their memory from under heaven. Never forget this!" (v. 19).

Later, however, when Saul had a chance to fulfill that command, he did not follow through. First Samuel 15 narrates the battle in which Saul defeated the Amalekites but did not finish them off. Indeed, it was not until Samuel arrived that their king, Agag, was executed.

Haman was a descendant of Agag, and Mordecai was

a descendant of Kish, the father of Saul (1 Sam. 9:1). In other words, the conflict between Mordecai and Haman is the story of unfinished business. The divine command of Exodus 17 and Deuteronomy 25 is finally carried out.

Interestingly, the book of Esther never once mentions the name of God. However, as in the highly similar book of Ruth, the reader more than understands that it is God who was behind these "coincidences" and reversals. God saved his people once again! This indeed was the occasion for a celebration.

Thus, Esther 9:20–32 establishes the celebration of Purim. It is named "lots" after the word used for the device that Haman and Ahasuerus used to determine the date for the slaughter of the Jewish people. Purim was a reminder that though God's people seemed to be in the hands of fate, they were really in the hands of God. Purim was an annual festival of joy and celebration.

According to modern custom, the story of Esther is read and whenever Haman's name is mentioned, boos follow, but cheers greet the name of Mordecai. The festival is also characterized by eating and drinking—indeed, the latter to such a point that one cannot tell the difference between Haman and Mordecai.

Purim was a biblical festival with a twist. The other festivals were celebrated in connection with the establishment of Israel as a nation and by divine decree. Purim was a celebration of the survival of the people of God.[1]

THE TRAJECTORY TO CHRIST

Purim celebrated the day that God reversed the fortunes of the Jewish people living in Persia. They were slated to die, but instead God used the occasion to defeat Israel's longtime enemy the Amalekites. God, through his providence, enacted redemption out of evil.

While there is no direct connection between Purim

and Christ, we see that the same principle was incarnated in his life and ministry. Evil men and women, and behind them Satan, wanted to see Jesus dead. This hatred took him to the cross. Peter, though, had these amazing words to say about the cross:

> People of Israel, listen! God publicly endorsed Jesus of Nazareth by doing wonderful miracles, wonders, and signs through him, as you well know. But you followed God's prearranged plan. With the help of lawless Gentiles, you nailed him to the cross and murdered him. However, God released him from the horrors of death and raised him back to life again, for death could not keep him in its grip. (Acts 2:22–24)

God overrules evil for our salvation. It is this great act that we celebrate, not on Purim, but throughout our lives.

FOR FURTHER REFLECTION

1. Purim celebrated God's providence in the lives of the Jewish people living in Persia. Where do you see God's providential hand working in your life?
2. We have also seen how God delivered the Jewish people by an act of ironic reversal at the time of Esther and also how he saved all of us through the death of Christ on the cross. As you reflect on your life, do you see any place where God has used the evil acts of others for good purposes?

POSTSCRIPT

G od reveals himself to his people through the pages of the Old Testament. We have taken a slice of this revelation, the priestly theology, in order to explore his nature and how he relates to his people. We have entered this world of ritual, however strange to us, thanks to the history-changing work of Jesus Christ. We have witnessed the divine King as he established sacred space, acts, people, and time in a sinful world. We have also marveled at the way that Jesus fulfilled this important aspect of Old Testament theology. This should not surprise us, because Christ himself said that he fulfilled the entirety of the Old Testament (Luke 24:25–27, 44–49).

Finally, we have been reminded of the central place of worship in the life of God's people. God has shaped his own worship, and he desires our praise.

NOTES

❧

Preface

1 See T. Longman III, *Making Sense of the Old Testament* (Grand Rapids: Baker, 1998).

CHAPTER ONE. PARADISE GAINED AND LOST: SACRED SPACE FROM THE BEGINNING

1 Specifically, Genesis 2:4b–25.
2 A translation of this may be found in J. Pritchard, *Ancient Near Eastern Texts* (Princeton: University of Princeton Press, 1969), 60–72.
3 Ibid., 104–6.
4 An illuminating and full study of Genesis 2–3 may be found in H. Wallace, *The Eden Narrative* (Atlanta: Scholars, 1985), though this reference should not be taken as an endorsement of all the author's methods or conclusions.
5 *New International Dictionary of Old Testament Theology and Exegesis*, ed. W. A. VanGemeren, 5 vols. (Grand Rapids: Zondervan, 1997), 4:555. This meaning suggests itself on the basis of an Aramaic cognate. Note also the important article by A. Millard, "The Etymology of Eden," *Vetus Testamentum* 34 (1984), 103–6.
6 G. Wenham, *Genesis 1–15* (Waco, Tex.: Word, 1987), 62–64; V. P. Hamilton, *Genesis 1–17* (Grand Rapids: Eerdmans, 1990), 162–66; K. A. Matthews, *Genesis 1–11:26* (Nashville: Broadman and Holman, 1996), 201–7.
7 See the summary description of this theme in T. Longman III and R. B. Dillard, *An Introduction to the Old Testament* (Grand Rapids: Zondervan, 1994), 52–53.

CHAPTER TWO. ALTARS: OCCASIONAL TESTIMONIES TO SACRED SPACE

1 I. Duguid, *Living in the Gap between Promise and Reality: The Gospel according to Abraham* (Phillipsburg, N.J.: P&R Publishing, 1999).

CHAPTER THREE. THE TABERNACLE OF MOSES: SACRED SPACE FOR THE LONG HAUL

1 T. Fretheim, *Exodus,* Interpretation: A Bible Commentary for Preaching and Teaching (Louisville: John Knox Press, 1991), 264.

2 As observed by R. W. Klein, "Back to the Future: The Tabernacle in the Book of Exodus," *Interpretation* 50 (1996): 264.

3 There is no question that the tabernacle is often referred to as a tent and occasionally as the Tent of Meeting, but there is a legitimate question as to whether at certain times there was a second Tent of Meeting in distinction to the tabernacle.

4 P. Kiene, *The Tabernacle of God in the Wilderness of Sinai* (Grand Rapids: Zondervan, 1977).

5 Ibid., 35.

6 Ibid., 34.

7 A good example of a writing with the clear intention to be an allegory is *Pilgrim's Progress,* the main character of which is called Christian, whose life journey takes him to places with names such as the Slough of Despond.

8 Notice the main difference between a symbolic and an allegorical interpretation. The latter has many different meanings; the symbolic interpretation focuses on one central meaning.

9 For a fuller development of these connections plus additional ones, see Fretheim, *Exodus,* 268–72.

10 J. D. Levenson, *Creation and the Persistence of Evil: The Jewish Drama of Divine Omnipotence* (Princeton: Princeton University Press, 1988), 86.

CHAPTER FIVE. THE FURNITURE OF THE SANCTUARY: AN INSIDE LOOK AT SACRED SPACE

1 I have found the work of M. Woudstra, *The Ark of the Covenant from Conquest to Kingship* (Philadelphia: Presbyterian and Reformed, 1965), very helpful.

2 M. Haran, *Temples and Temple Service in Ancent Israel: An Inquiry into Biblical Cult Phenomena and the Historical Setting of the Priestly School* (Winona Lake, Ind.: Eisenbrauns, 1985), 276–88.

3 R. W. Klein, "Back to the Future: The Tabernacle in the Book of Exodus," *Interpretation* 50 (1996): 268.

4 V. Poythress, *The Shadow of Christ in the Law of Moses* (1991, reprint, Phillipsburg, N.J.: P&R Publishing, 1995), 18–19.

5 So C. Meyers, "Realms of Sanctity: The Case of the 'Misplaced' Incense Altar in the Tabernacle Texts of Exodus," in *Texts, Tem-*

ples, and Traditions, ed. M. V. Fox et al. (Winona Lake, Ind.: Eisenbrauns, 1996), 33–46.

6 Lev. 4:7 talks about how some of the blood is also put on the horns of the incense altar within the tabernacle (see above).

7 This ritual, of course, would not take all the animal's blood, and so the text goes on to say that the rest was poured at the base of the altar (e.g. Lev. 4:34).

CHAPTER SIX. THE COMING OF IMMANUEL: WHERE DO CHRISTIANS FIND HOLY SPACE?

1 Interestingly, the Samaritans had their own version of the Pentateuch (not surprisingly called today the "Samaritan Pentateuch"). In the passages where God instructs his people as to the place of proper worship, the Samaritan Pentateuch has substituted Gerizim for Sinai.

2 Or, as G. Guthrie (*Hebrews,* NIV Application Commentary [Grand Rapids: Zondervan, 1998], 20) puts it as he discusses the original hearers of the epistle, "Prior to accepting Christ the worship orientation of these believers had been to the synagogue."

CHAPTER SEVEN. THE 'OLAH: THE WHOLE BURNT OFFERING

1 It is true, nonetheless, that sacrifice occurred before Sinai, indeed as early as right after the Fall (Gen. 4). As a matter of fact, the Hebrew term for altar, the place where pre-Mosaic people of God worshiped the Lord, means etymologically "place of sacrifice," indicating that sacrifice took place long before Moses.

2 Among commentaries, I have found M. F. Rooker, *Leviticus,* New American Commentary (Nashville: Broadman and Holman, 2000) particularly helpful.

3 For more on the connection between treaty and covenant, see T. Longman III, *Reading the Bible with Head and Mind* (Colorado Springs: NavPress, 1997), 121–27.

4 In fact, according to Rooker (*Leviticus,* 91), evidence indicates that the sacrifice of a sheep was the most common type of *'olah.*

5 The sacrifice is called the *minhah* here. In the next section we will discuss the *minhah* as it is described in Leviticus 2; however, in contexts like Genesis 4 it appears that *minhah* can be used as a term to "sacrifice" in general.

6 B. Waltke ("Cain and His Offering," *Westminster Theological Journal* 48 (1985): 363–72) has shown how the issue is not a matter of a blood versus a nonblood sacrifice.

CHAPTER EIGHT. THE MINHAH AND SHELAMIM: TRIBUTE AND FELLOWSHIP OFFERINGS

1 Translation from J. C. L. Gibson, *Canaanite Myths and Legends* (1978), p. 42, lines 37–38, quoted in the *New International Dictionary of Old Testament Theology and Exegesis,* ed. W. A. VanGemeren, 5 vols. (Grand Rapids: Zondervan, 1997), 2:979.

2 See also Lev. 21:6 and Num. 28:2.

3 W. Eichrodt, *Theology of the Old Testament* (Westminster, 1961), 1:143–44, quoted by M. F. Rooker, *Leviticus,* New American Commentary (Nashville: Broadman and Holman, 2000), 103.

4 So argues Rooker, *Leviticus,* 102.

CHAPTER NINE. THE HATTAT AND ASHAM: SIN AND GUILT OFFERINGS

1 J. Milgrom, *Leviticus 1–16,* Anchor Bible, vol. 3 (Garden City, N.Y.: Doubleday, 1991), 373.

2 M. F. Rooker, *Leviticus,* New American Commentary (Nashville: Broadman and Holman, 2000), 111.

3 G. J. Wenham, *The Book of Leviticus,* New International Commentary on the Old Testament (Grand Rapids: Eerdmans, 1979), 103–12; Milgrom, *Leviticus 1–16,* 319–77.

CHAPTER TEN. CHRIST: THE ONCE-AND-FOR-ALL SACRIFICE!

1 Commentators on Romans 3:25 discuss the issue of whether the Greek word here (*hilastērion*) means "mercy seat" as the place of propitiation (or turning away the wrath of God) or propitiatory/expiatory sacrifice. I obviously agree with the majority of modern interpreters in taking it in the second sense. For details, see D. Moo, *Romans 1–8* (Chicago: Moody Press, 1991), 231–42; J. Murray, *Epistle to the Romans,* New International Commentary on the New Testament (Grand Rapids: Eerdmans, 1959), 116–21, though the recent doctoral dissertation by D. P. Bailey, *Jesus as the Mercy Seat: The Semantics and Theology of Paul's Use of Hilasterion in Romans 3:25* (University of Cambridge, 1999) would disagree. J. D. G. Dunn, *Romans 1–8*, Word Biblical Commentary (Dallas: Word, 1988), 180–82, makes a strong case that this Greek word used for the mercy seat in the Septuagint, implies the sacrifice in the Holy of Holies on the Day of Atonement. See also the discussion of *hilasmos* in 1 John below.

2 Here we cite the NIV because the NLT, which I have been citing throughout, falls short in the rendering of this phrase in Lev. 1. It

obscures the reference to smell with its translation "very pleasing to the LORD."

3 See G. Burge, *Letters of John,* NIV Application Commentary (Grand Rapids: Zondervan, 1996), 85–86.

4 See G. Guthrie, *Hebrews,* NIV Application Commentary (Grand Rapids: Zondervan, 1998), 440.

CHAPTER ELEVEN. THE RISE OF THE PRIESTHOOD

1 See part one, on the altar.

2 Also known as Reuel (Exod. 2:18; Num. 10:29) and Hobab (Judg. 4:11), though there may be a textual problem here (cf. Num. 10:29).

3 C. F. Keil and F. Delitzsch, *The Pentateuch,* vol. 2 in Commentary on the Old Testament (Grand Rapids: Eerdmans, 1949), 102, offers the suggestion that there was a caste of priests before the specific consecration of Aaron and the Levites. This, of course, is possible, but is pure speculation. P. Enns, *Exodus,* NIV Application Commentary (Grand Rapids: Zondervan, 1999), 393–95, also expresses difficulty with this reference and suggests either an otherwise unknown pre-Aaronic priesthood or chronological displacement.

4 So P. Jenson, *"khn,"* in *New International Dictionary of Old Testament Theology and Exegesis,* ed. W. A. VanGemeren, 5 vols. (Grand Rapids: Zondervan, 1997), 2:601.

5 See M. Kline, *Images of the Spirit* (privately published, 1980), 42–47.

6 We here are describing the high priestly ephod. Other priests wore a simple linen ephod, and there are some passages (e.g., 1 Sam. 23:1–6) that imply that a metallic ephod was used for divinatory purposes. Alternatively for the latter, the ephod, connected to the breastpiece that contained the Urim and Thummim, may simply have been an indirect way of referring to the Urim and Thummim.

7 M. Haran, *Temples and Temple Service in Ancent Israel: An Inquiry into Biblical Cult Phenomena and the Historical Setting of the Priestly School* (Winona Lake, Ind.: Eisenbrauns, 1985), 214–15.

8 As expressed by Lev. 8:4, "So Moses followed the LORD's instructions." J. E. Hartley, *Leviticus,* Word Biblical Commentary (Dallas: Word, 1992), 109, points out that "for the most part the wording of these two accounts [Exod. 29 and Lev. 8] is so similar that one passage is dependent on the other or both adhered closely to a common source."

CHAPTER TWELVE. LEVITES AND THE PRIESTLY LIFE STYLE

1 I was helped in this section by G. Wenham, *The Book of Leviticus,* New International Commentary on the Old Testament (Grand Rapids: Eerdmans, 1979), 288–97.

CHAPTER THIRTEEN. PRIESTLY SERVICE: GOD'S BODYGUARDS

1 J. A. Naude, *"nzr,"* in *New International Dictionary of Old Testament Theology and Exegesis,* ed. W. A. VanGemeren, 5 vols. (Grand Rapids: Zondervan, 1997), 3:74.

CHAPTER FOURTEEN. JESUS, THE ULTIMATE PRIEST

1 For a survey of the theme of Christ as a priestly figure from the perspective of a theologian, see the excellent study by J. Wilson, *God So Loved the World: A Christology for Disciples* (Grand Rapids: Baker, 2001).

2 I have benefited greatly from reading the treatment of Hebrews 7 found in O. P. Robertson, *The Israel of God: Yesterday, Today, and Tomorrow* (Phillipsburg, N.J.: P&R Publishing, 2000), 53–83.

CHAPTER FIFTEEN. THE SABBATH: THE FOCUS OF SACRED TIME

1 For fuller studies from different perspectives, see D. A. Carson, *From Sabbath to Lord's Day* (Grand Rapids: Zondervan, 1982); M. J. Dawn, *Keeping the Sabbath Wholly: Ceasing, Resting, Embracing* (Grand Rapids: Eerdmans, 1989); N.-E. A. Andreasen, *Rest and Redemption: A Study of the Biblical Sabbath* (Berrien Springs, Mich.: Andrews University Press, 1978); J. Douma, *The Ten Commandments: A Manual for the Christian Life,* trans. N. D. Kloosterman (Phillipsburg, N.J.: P&R Publishing, 1996), 109–60.

2 We can see this also in Exod. 23:10–13 and Num. 28:9–10, which list the sacrifices offered at sacred times, starting with daily offerings, but then continuing with the Sabbath, before going on to the other festivals. Deut. 16 is a shorter list, including only the three pilgrimage festivals: Passover, Weeks, and Tabernacles.

3 It is true that this etymology has been questioned and others put forward, but in my estimation, the explanation just given is the best hypothesis. See discussion in *New International Dictionary of Old Testament Theology and Exegesis,* ed. W. A. VanGemeren, 5 vols. (Grand Rapids: Zondervan, 1997), 4:1156.

4 We will explore this further later, but for an extensive discussion, see my *Reading the Bible with Heart and Mind* (Colorado Springs: NavPress, 1997), 113–28.

5 See examples, in J. Pritchard, *Ancient Near Eastern Texts* (Princeton: Princeton University Press, 1969), 201–6. M. G. Kline, *Treaty of the Great King* (Grand Rapids: Eerdmans, 1963) is one of the most accessible introductions to the relationship between biblical covenants and ancient Near Eastern treaties.

6 See above, p. 165.

7 After all, though Gen. 2:18–25 clearly establishes monogamous marriage at creation, God permits a man to have many wives according to the Old Testament. The Mosaic law does not prohibit, but simply regulates a man's having many wives (see Exod. 21:7–11).

8 There is a debate as to whether the Jubilee year *followed* the seventh seventh year, resulting in two fallow years, or the Jubilee *was* the seventh seventh year. For an extensive discussion of this issue, plus an excellent explanation of Lev. 25 in detail, consult J. E. Hartley, *Leviticus,* Word Biblical Commentary (Dallas: Word, 1992), 415–48.

CHAPTER SIXTEEN. CHRIST AND SABBATH: SACRED TIME RECONFIGURED

1 Concerning Jesus' reference to the high priest at this time as Abiathar rather than Ahimelech, see D. E. Garland, *Mark,* NIV Application Commentary (Grand Rapids: Zondervan, 1996), 106.

2 The new-moon festival is also mentioned in the Old Testament as a regularly occurring day on which special sacrifices were offered (see Num. 28:11; Isa. 1:13). The new moon marked the beginning of the month.

3 For this reason, some scholars feel that the trumpet call that will announce Christ's final return (Matt. 24:31; 1 Cor. 15:52; 1 Thess. 4:16) is specifically to be connected to the trumpet that announces the beginning of the ultimate Sabbath of the Old Testament, the year of Jubilee.

CHAPTER SEVENTEEN. THE HAGGIM (PILGRIMAGE FESTIVALS): MORE ON SACRED TIME

1 K. Kitchen, "The Exodus," *Anchor Bible Dictionary,* ed. D. N. Freedman (Garden City, N.Y.: Doubleday, 1992), 2:702.

2 B. Waltke, "The Date of the Conquest," *Westminster Theological Journal* 52 (1990): 200.

3 Other texts relevant for this summary of the Passover and Unleavened Bread Festival include Exod. 23:15; 34:18; Lev. 23:4–8; Num. 9:1–15; 28:16–25; 33:3; Deut. 16:1–8; Josh. 5:10–12; 2 Kings 23:21–30; 2 Chron. 30:1–27; 35:1–9; Ezra 6:19–22; Ezek. 45:21.

4 One possible original meaning of *pesah* is "limp" or "skip." While some take this to indicate a type of dance performed at the festival, it may be related to the idea that the angel of death skips over the households of Israel on this fateful night.

5 T. D. Alexander, *From Paradise to Promised Land* (Carlisle, England: Paternoster Press, 1997), 78.

6 For more detail on the interpretation of the Song of Songs, see T. Longman III, *Song of Songs,* New International Commentary on the Old Testament (Grand Rapids: Eerdmans, 2001).

7 I agree with the statement of T. D. Alexander ("The Passover Sacrifice," in *Sacrifice in the Bible,* ed. R. T. Beckwith and M. J. Selman [Grand Rapids: Baker, 1995], 3): "Because they cannot be substantiated, traditio-historical theories about the Passover's origin must be treated with the utmost caution."

8 J. E. Hartley, *Leviticus,* Word Biblical Commentary (Dallas: Word, 1992), 383–84.

9 And in this passage we get yet another name for the festival, namely "firstfruits." This probably indicates its close connection with the waving of the first grain sheaf mentioned in Lev. 23.

CHAPTER EIGHTEEN. FESTIVALS OF TRUMPETS AND THE DAY OF ATONEMENT: VERY SPECIAL SACRED TIMES

1 See the helpful comments by J. E. Hartley, *Leviticus,* Word Biblical Commentary (Dallas: Word, 1992), 387.

2 However, we should perhaps understand that the trumpets (in this case *hatsotsera*) are the two silver trumpets described in Num. 10:1–10.

3 See pp. 122–24.

4 For description and discussion of significance, see pp. 124–26.

CHAPTER NINETEEN. PURIM: LATECOMER TO SACRED TIME

1 In this way it is similar to Hanukkah, a celebration of the deliverance of the Jewish people from the oppression of Antiochus IV in the middle of the second century B.C. Though this is a stirring story, we will not discuss this festival here or any other post-biblical Jewish festival.

INDEX OF SCRIPTURE